Love Centered Parenting

Contributing to Your Child's Wellness by Living From
The Heart and Cultivating Your Inner Wisdom

Maria Gavriel

BALBOA.
PRESS
A DIVISION OF HAY HOUSE

Balboa Press books may be ordered through booksellers or by contacting:

Balboa Press
A Division of Hay House
1663 Liberty Drive
Bloomington, IN 47403
www.balboapress.com
1 (877) 407-4847

Because of the dynamic nature of the Internet, any web addresses or links contained in this book may have changed since publication and may no longer be valid. The views expressed in this work are solely those of the author and do not necessarily reflect the views of the publisher, and the publisher hereby disclaims any responsibility for them.

The following recommendations are based on my personal experiences, education and opinions, and are not to be considered as a substitute for consultation, diagnosis, or treatment with a licensed health practitioner.

Any people depicted in stock imagery provided by Thinkstock are models, and such images are being used for illustrative purposes only.
Certain stock imagery © Thinkstock.

Printed in the United States of America.

ISBN: 978-1-4525-2336-1 (sc)
ISBN: 978-1-4525-2338-5 (hc)
ISBN: 978-1-4525-2337-8 (e)

Library of Congress Control Number: 2014918227

Balboa Press rev. date: 10/22/2014

Contents

Foreword
By Dr. Pina LoGiudice, ND, Lac

M any of my patients confide in me how they wish their children came with an instructional manual. Well, finally one is here! *Love Centered Parenting* by Maria Gavriel is what every parent has been looking for, the outstanding guide every parent should own, to support the most important job in the world: raising a happy and healthy child.

I first met Maria as a fellow parent, bringing our children to the pre-kindergarten program at the Waldorf School of Garden City, New York. As a naturopathic physician and mother, I was immediately drawn to her energy and the thoughtfulness she brought to parenting. The more I get to know her, the more I am fascinated by her journey, both as a parent and as someone destined to help scores of new parents. I am inspired by her passion to bring holistic parenting to the forefront of our lives.

In *Love Centered Parenting,* Maria does a tremendous job by offering parents simple, practical advice that we can all use. This is advice that works, whether you have a newborn or a teenager. She beautifully describes all aspects of her journey--from fertility issues, to the birth process, and even to conflict resolution with her child. Maria honestly and open-heartedly discusses her trials and tribulations as a new mother. She takes on the small issues, and the biggies, with a balanced and sensible approach enriched with a nurturing spirit throughout. Whether discussing choices for toys, foods, or vaccines, she presents clear and researched information in a non-dogmatic, non-judgmental and caring manner, that allows readers to consider what may be best for their particular situation. Throughout this work, she openly invites you as a parent, or as any person interested in healthful living and holistic parenting, to mindfully cultivate your own unique parenting style. At the same time, she offers invaluable advice on how to connect spiritually with your child and the environment around your family.

As a naturopathic physician, I am always expressing to my patients the need to return to a more holistic way of life to prevent disease, allow the body to heal itself, and to ultimately bring us to our greatest health potential. In this spirit, I continually prescribe meditation, organic foods, minimizing environmental toxins, connecting with nature, exercising, and using natural remedies designed not to cover up symptoms, but instead, to help the body balance itself. *Love Centered Parenting* beautifully parallels and expands on this paradigm. This book clearly lays out a plan that is manageable, effective, and life-affirming.

The world is finally looking for, and realizing the value of holistic thinking. As the universe would have it, I was the first naturopathic physician to appear on *The Dr. Oz Show, The Katie Couric Show,* and many national news networks. I can tell you that while there are now many more people interested in this way of thinking and healing, there are also powerful opposing forces and people who feel threatened (politically, ideologically and financially) by what will become the new paradigm of medicine and health. Maria's book serves as an important foundation and resource for our generation, helping to ensure that this common-sense, healthy approach is fully and lovingly applied to the next generation.

Maria's journey is truly a testament to the fact that health and healing can occur at any stage of life, using natural medicine and intelligent mindfulness. The example of her journey offers us the secret of how to deeply connect with and understand our children, so they can gracefully, healthfully, and calmly develop into profound human beings--people who will traverse their lives successfully, in a heart-centered way, bringing their values with them throughout the world. As a mom and a physician, I thank you, Maria for this gift.

In love and light, with many continuing blessings,

Dr. Pina LoGiudice, ND, Lac

Dr. Pina LoGiudice is an acupuncturist and naturopathic physician, practicing in New York City at Inner Source Health. She is widely recognized by the media as an expert in the field of natural medicine, has published many articles, and is a co-author of *Textbook of Natural Medicine.* Her website is www.innersourcehealth.com.

Preface

Ten years ago, when I first began my journey to parenthood, I had no idea what kind of mother I would be, nor what lay before me. I didn't know that the journey would lead me to question everything I knew about myself, my health, parenting, and our family's way of life. Along the way, I discovered ways to reclaim my health that allowed me to conceive, and found the courage to forge my own path to a natural way of parenting.

Since then, my children have transformed my life. They have helped me grow to understand who I truly am and to trust myself, my family, and God. I've realized that I am simply their guide, and that their paths should be respected. In realizing this responsibility, I owe it to myself, to them, and to the world to heal myself on all levels so that I can guide and parent lovingly and honestly. This experience ultimately grants me the opportunity to continue learning from their presence and grow as a person.

I have come to know that parenting is one of the most important roles we have in life: raising another human being, guiding them, teaching them all we have come to know about the world. In years from now when I look back, I sincerely hope that I've done this well, so that my young apprentices can go forth on their journeys with as much ease, growth, and delight as possible.

I am still amazed by how little preparation we receive for such an extraordinary responsibility. In our society today, many professions require us to spend almost a decade in school to ensure that we are knowledgeable and well trained before we go to practice law, for example. We want to "do it right" and without a whole lot of negative repercussions.

With parenting, on the other hand, there is no training, schooling, or master apprenticeship—absolutely nothing to truly prepare us for the biggest responsibility we have as human beings. Aside from maybe attending a birthing class, a weekend workshop, and reading a few interesting parenting books, the truth is that we simply dive in, truly overnight; we are handed our child and off we go. And we cross our fingers and certainly hope for the best!

Well, if it wasn't specialized training that taught us (since the beginning of time) how to parent, other factors must have helped us, so that we could survive and thrive as a species today. Throughout history, we have been guided in this role through an Inner Guidance System, like a GPS, based on intuition, mother's wisdom, God, or whatever you choose to call it, and this has allowed humans to survive. This inner voice has been gifted to every single person, and is what one mother uses to guide another.

However, recent developments in our modern culture have lowered the volume on this inner voice, and have made it so hard to hear that we as parents no longer know which direction to follow. What exactly has been muffling that inner voice?

To me, life seems so complex, with so many more choices presented to us today, that we can easily find ourselves disillusioned and confused. When you are in the midst of parenting, each day seems to pass by so quickly that we have little time to reflect, wonder, connect, or question exactly what our actions and roles as parents should be. We trust our own intuition less and less, and allow our doubts, fears, and the external environment to guide almost every decision we make. We have lost that clear connection with our inner voice. So we feel that we must conform to what we hear from so-called experts, especially in the media—and if we do not conform, and choose to take a more natural approach to parenting, often we are treated like social outcasts.

Viewing ourselves as outcasts, we feel even more helpless and vulnerable, no longer able to trust our own inner guidance. And while we are in this state of vulnerability and confusion, we begin trusting others to make decisions for us and our children-because we believe that somehow they must know better. We seek out "expert advice" from our pediatricians, books, and the Internet, only to be left even more confused than when we first began-especially when these experts disagree with one another. What makes someone a parenting expert anyway?

There are plenty of experts on the subject of parenting out there. Instead of labeling myself an expert, too, I would rather describe myself as a parent who simply enjoys being helpful and supportive, and sharing my parenting success stories, failures, and challenges. I love to communicate what I've learned about how to get through the day and embrace all the challenges, love, and joy in every moment of parenting. The most important thing I can share with any parent is how to tune into yourself, your child, and the wisdom of the universe. Once you are attuned, all else comes much easier.

Although I have learned to tune in better, it wasn't always this way. There was a road of self-exploration that I traveled, and I took baby steps to get to where I am today. When I was a new mom, I very soon realized that my parenting style was "different." Through more experience and being part of a community, I now realize that I fit into the categories of wholistic parent, Attachment Parenting (AP parent), natural mom, organic mom, and all the other terms that the mainstream uses today to describe parents who choose to raise their children more closely to the way nature intended.

During my first go at parenting, I remember searching for a book or other sources that I could relate to, but unfortunately, there weren't many available that I found helpful. I truly wished I could have found a book (or website) that was written by a mom—one who could have encouraged me to trust my intuition, teach me how to hear my inner voice, and trust my own style of mothering first, before anyone else's advice.

Recently I have found many wonderful examples of parenting literature, which I will refer to throughout the book (and which can be found in the resource section). Almost all of them focus on one specific aspect or style of parenting. Many are written by brilliant men, who provide illuminating and scientifically accurate information. However, what I really longed for was guidance written by regular, everyday moms, whose advice is just as grounded in experience as it is in intuition.

Recently, the "wholistic movement" has grown dramatically, and you are able to find good blogs, magazines, networks, support groups, and communities that help support parents and their ideas and decisions about raising their children. The wholistic movement to me is a way of life that is aligned with nature and who I truly am. This includes every aspect of life, such as diet, health care, daily action, and mostly living life from a place of Truth – meaning that I try to do what feels right deep within me. More and more people are able to live from this space as they flex their intuition muscles. And through others, I feel supported to be able to do this more and more. It is through each parent's simple sharing of their experiences and offering of support that the answers come shining through. I offer my experience and advice in this spirit.

This is the book that I once wished had been available to me. I hope that it can help you to find your own inner wisdom and to hear it loudly and clearly, and then find the community and research to support you. This book began humbly, with me writing down my parenting experiences, in hopes that they would support you on your own parenting journey. You'll hear about my fertility challenges, my experiences of pregnancy, birth, breastfeeding, sleep issues, diet, natural healing, healthy toys and clothing, and how I am still learning to trust myself when it comes to raising my children.

I will end most chapters with a meditation to help you center and connect with yourself. I want you to find your own interpretation of the topic covered in the chapter, and assimilate what feels authentic to you. You will witness the evolution in my parenting lifestyle, and how the combination of intuition with a supportive community and holistic information has helped me and my family to arrive at where we are today. And we are still learning (since we never graduate from this experience). As I share all I've learned, I invite you to come on the adventure with me and look over my shoulder. I hope that my story inspires you to discover a path to parenting that is authentic to you, to understand who you are as a parent, and to practice instinctual and holistic childrearing in the midst of our busy modern world.

I always begin my conversations with parents by saying, "Well, this is what worked for us and I hope this helps you." And that is how I shall begin this book.

May you embark on your journey with an open heart.

> *"Why should we ever go abroad, even across the way, to ask a neighbor's advice? There is a nearer neighbor within us incessantly telling us how we should behave."*
>
> – Henry David Thoreau

Acknowledgments

I am in awe that I have finally finished a book I never planned to birth. After two years of love and labor, I offer it to the world. It all began with my son asking me to write a children's book with him. I am grateful to him for sparking this book, and for my daughter's inspiration to share my stories with the world. I wish to express my appreciation for my husband's loving support, excitement, and encouragement throughout the process. It is thanks to my family and their contribution in my life that I even have a story to share.

I cherish my parents for being my biggest teachers, for all their love and for a beautiful childhood. To my (soul) sister Olga, whose unconditional love and life long presence is a gift and a rare treasure. For Maria, Irene and all my beautiful friendships, I am forever thankful for their endless love. To all of my mom friends and communities, whose presence, honesty, love, and support is as powerful, and necessary as any women's tribe.

Thank you to all the doctors, practitioners and healers that dare to step out of the modern medical paradigm to offer healthcare to their patients with dedication, wisdom, expertise, and true diligence. It is because of the support that I receive from an empowering practitioner network, that I can trust and honor my own healing abilities for myself and my family.

Special thanks to my editor Phyllis Stern for her patience and for gently guiding me through my first editing process while piecing the work together with her knowledge and experience. I am thankful to my fun friend and editor, Judie Harvey for pouring a loving polish over the final material.

To all my mentors, teachers and guides, I thank you for your love, dedication and commitment to my transformation.

My heart is filled with gratitude to our Creator, for the possibility of this life experience and for all that I am.

PART I

Inviting a Child

CHAPTER 1

How It All Began

I am currently a very happy mother of two little angels, who give my life direction. When I first began writing this book, my son was four and a half (never forget that half) and my daughter was twenty-one months old. Every time I sat down to write, they were at the core of each message. I was just like any other mother out there, trying to keep it all together, while at the same time figuring it all out as I went—juggling my many roles, including mothering, parenting, advancing my career, keeping up the house, and doing my best to be a loving spouse.

Despite the sometimes frenetic lifestyle, I am very happy to be a mother. However, ten years ago, if you had broached the subject of motherhood with me, I would have said that the thought was almost nonexistent to me. I was consumed with plans for traveling and for exploring myself, my husband, my life, and our world. Ideally, I could have become a geologist studying rocks up on a Swiss mountaintop with my professor, maybe lived at a Buddhist monastery in Asia, or perhaps extended my time with the Peace Corps.

Suddenly however, in the midst of being high on love, and inhaling the Southern Californian air, I somehow had the urge to have children. It crept up on me in a way that changed my life and who I would be forever, as you can imagine. Interestingly, I felt I had to become reacquainted with myself all over again: "Hello Maria, so nice to meet you…"

What's the Hold Up?

Being married to a gym addict, I thought I knew how to keep my body healthy and fit. I trained in the gym four days a week, had my protein shakes after my workout, enjoyed my yoga on the weekends, biked once a week, did martial arts once a week, and enjoyed enough hiking to last me a lifetime. I was in pretty great shape. At least it looked that way from the outside. Healthy enough, I thought, until I moved back to New York and began trying to have my first child. Because I thought there was no reason why we would not conceive right away, since I was fit and thought I was living a healthy lifestyle, I made sure that we were ready for this major step in our lives. I had to make sure for myself that our life was in a state to include children, because I was under the impression that we would have one immediately, and life would change overnight.

After six months of trying, I began to wonder if we were doing something wrong. I mean, throughout my relationship we were always careful to prevent pregnancy, because we were not quite ready to take such a big step. So why now, just when we were actually intending to have a child, wasn't it happening? Well, I figured that the answer was just to have more sex, like every single day, maybe more than once, and… eventually one of those little guys would make it to my egg. But after we did that unsuccessfully for another six months, I decided to talk to my gynecologist about our situation. Could there be something wrong with one of us?

My gynecologist suggested that since we had been trying for a year, I should go have my tubes "flushed out" by the blue ink dye test, known medically as the hysterosalpingogram, and better known as the HSG test. I wondered, what did that mean? I was willing to do whatever my doctor said, and so I went, only to go through one of the most painful procedures, just to be told my fallopian tubes were not clogged and my uterus was fine, too. At least I left feeling a bit more optimistic. The nurse explained that once a woman's tubes were flushed out by this dye, most conceive right away. I thought, how exciting.

But after trying for another six months, back to my doctor I went. I was feeling pretty bummed out at this point. "What is going on?" I asked. And after the doctor attempted to comfort me, he suggested that I see a specialist. After much research, and asking around, I got the courage to visit a very well-known fertility specialist in Manhattan. The one-hour trek from my home once a month was difficult, but at that point, I was willing to do anything in order to figure out what was "wrong" with me or us, simply to have our long-awaited child.

After my first consultation, my husband and I were told that we would be checked out thoroughly by going through a complete physical and medical assessment. The doctor also cautioned that the tests don't always find the reason why a couple can't conceive naturally. In an attempt to be supportive, he suggested we begin to think seriously of in-vitro as an option and to consider storing and freezing my eggs. The doctor told us much more than we were able to take in at the moment, and it was really hard for both of us.

My husband and I went home and talked about this for days. We found the subject draining and slightly depressing. Regardless, we decided to go ahead with the medical check-up, because we really just wanted to have a child already—and had been ready for over a year. The scenario had already begun to suck the life out of us, and we were not sure how much more we could take.

The following month, bright and early, my husband was handed a magazine and a cup, and was instructed to go into a closet-sized room and fill the cup with his little swimmers. Some time later, we were informed that my husband actually had "super sperm," and all was very healthy on his part. Wonderful news—I was next.

The next month, I had my ovaries tested and my blood work done, along with several other procedures that I believe my brain somehow deleted in order for me to be strong enough to go through all of what was ahead of me. A few days later, I got the great news that I was also very healthy and capable of conceiving and carrying a child. Yay!

Although this news should have been exciting, and maybe even reassuring, actually, it was far from that. Could anyone explain what the hell was going on here? Even more depressing, I began to experience constant anxiety, wondering if this month was going to be a huge success or another disappointing failure for us. I was so consumed with having a child that this was all I thought of, all that my life revolved around. This was not fun anymore.

For the next few months I had my blood work done once a day, every single month, to know exactly when I was ovulating. If I was, we were given a cup to fill the next morning with my husband's magic potion. And on those mornings we would have sex, fill up the cup, drive for an hour to the clinic, have the sperm inserted into my uterus, and pray, hope and keep our fingers crossed that this would be the time that our baby would decide to enter our universe, through my womb. My heart would pound so loudly—as I waited for an eternity for the sonogram technician to check my uterus to see if a sperm and egg had implanted—that I was sure he could hear my heart beating. Months went by like this, and every month, the news was even more discouraging.

One day, I was called to make an appointment to see the specialist, who informed me that there was no reason to keep going this route, and that I should now begin injecting myself with the pharmaceutical drug Clomid. This would increase the number of eggs I produced every month, in other words increase the number of targets that my husband's sperm would have. I almost began to cry, and I could not believe that I was on the path of having to go through in-vitro fertilization. I never would have thought that I would be unable to conceive. I could not stop thinking that there was something wrong, and that no one had been able to identify it.

I went to the pharmacist with a huge rock in my throat, got my shots, and began injecting Clomid into my uterus, as instructed. When I went back a few weeks later, my sonogram showed something for the very first time. How exciting! The technician wouldn't tell me exactly what it showed on the screen, but again, I was led into the specialist's office and sat in his awful chair. "What can it be now?" I thought.

I recall him saying to me, "The Clomid has created a large cyst on your ovary, and you must stop any attempt to conceive a child until it goes away."

I felt my face begin to heat up. And then I exploded. "I've done everything you have told me to do. There is nothing wrong with either me or my husband, and *now* you're telling me I can't even try to conceive due to the medication you put me on? And if that's not bad enough, you are not sure how long it will take for the cyst to go away? Your advice is to 'simply wait and see'? Are you seriously having this conversation with me?"

After I lost my lid in his office, I stormed out, returned the remaining injections to the pharmacy, and went home. I should have followed my gut and never gone down this path. Now what was I to do?

A Moment of Despair and Feeling Lost

I went home and called my childhood friend and confident, Olga, and vented to her about my whole experience with the fertility clinic and the specialist, and how it just did not feel right for me personally. Although I knew we wanted a baby, I also knew that it was just as important to me to have the element of magic and surprise, instead of all this technology and elaborate dissection of baby making. Not that there is anything wrong with it at all, which is why I even tried that route. Many parents are very grateful for in vitro technology. It was just not right for me personally, since magic and spirit have been a constant part of my life, for as long as I can remember.

And so I couldn't understand why this magic was not happening with conceiving our child. As my best friend heard my complaining about all this for the fiftieth time, she paused as usual, and then spoke from the heart with a response that truly resonated within me. Her response allowed me to be able to take a deep breath, and my body eased up for the first time in years. She said that my child was in the heavens, simply waiting for the perfect time to arrive. He is making his travels to us, and he knows we have invited him, but something has held him back. When the time is right, he would join us. Nothing could have been truer than what she said. After all, she should know—she is my son's godmother.

Our Gateway to a New Way of Life

Well, why was he not joining us already? I wondered if my unborn child had a purpose as we all do. Maybe…when he chose to come into our realm, he made certain decisions about what purpose he was to fulfill, and what hardships he would face during this process. I feel that my son knew what kind of home and global environment he was coming into. In fact, my son began schooling me before he even got here. Honestly, both of my children created the life that I lead today. If it wasn't for my first born having me wait all this time, and for overcoming all of our fertility challenges, I would never have realized that I wasn't truly honoring my body. Through this journey I was led to my acupuncturist Michael Gaeta DAc, MS, CDN —our gateway to this lifestyle—who helped me see how to eat and live in a more wholistic way. Once my body, my environment, and my life were in a much healthier state, our child knew it was time to join us.

Michael came into my life at the perfect time. I had heard of an acupuncturist, who was very well known for helping women, including his own wife, to conceive. I met Michael right before all went sour with the fertility specialist. I remember that during my first conversation with him, I had been thrown off by his subtle suggestion that my body might be toxic. I thought that he simply did not know how well I had been taking care of my body, and that he simply didn't have the details about what I had gone through to make sure I was "healthy." So of course, I proceeded to explain myself, and his response was simply life-altering. Dr. Gaeta spent the next two hours helping me understand that everything that I had been through had burdened my body with toxins, and that he believed that once all this toxicity was cleared from my body, I would be able to conceive. It would take a lot of work and commitment from both our ends to reach this goal. I wasn't quite sure what this work involved yet.

> Currently, the term *holistic* is used more loosely and can have a range of meaning. Throughout the book, you will notice *wholistic* and *holistic* used. Whenever you see the word *wholistic* it means the whole human (mind, body and spirit). The word *holistic* is used when referring to organic food, supplements, and alternative natural methods or products.

For the first time I realized that my body had been bombarded with chemicals for years, starting with the synthetic and highly toxic vitamin-store supplements, harmful synthetic vitamins, cancerous protein drinks, so-called "natural" skin care products, diet, clothing, and many other things. "Overwhelmed" is not the word for what I felt when I left the office. If it wasn't for that initial acupuncture treatment, and the inexplicable trust that I had for this man, I would have never returned. But I did, once a week for a year.

There were so many other concerns that he also helped me, my husband and children with, and the more he helped us and improved our life and our health, the more he felt like family to us. He became our "go to" person for illnesses, my husband's acid reflux, my fractured bone, my children's colic, and much more.

Meditation

Find a quiet moment in your day. If you can't find it, request it of yourself so that you allow yourself to create one. Maybe first thing in the morning, or the last part of your day. Close your eyes and take slow deep breaths. Inhale through your nose and exhale through your mouth. When thoughts arise, notice them, let them go, and return to your breath. After several breaths, when you feel calmer, slowly return to your normal breathing.

Visualize a beam of blue light being shined down on you from above. You are encased in this beam of blue light. Hold this vision for a while.

While you are enjoying this bath of blue light, visualize your heart projecting a golden light full of love down towards your uterus. Fill your uterus with love and golden light. Hold this vision also for a while.

Repeat once a day or as often as possible.

CHAPTER 2

Clean-Up Time

S o how exactly did this wholistic lifestyle evolve for me? Well, I first began by cleaning out all my products, such as those for body, skin, and hair care, and replacing them with toxin-free products. I found that this was not easy, initially because of the difference in cost for each product, and then because many items that are labeled "natural" are truly far from it. My suggestion here is to educate yourself about those large chemical-sounding and scientific words written in small fonts under the "ingredients" section of your products. To keep it simple, if you can't say the word, then just stay away from it. And "environmentally friendly," unfortunately, does not mean non-toxic. You will find that although there is a selection, there are actually not as many products out there that are truly pure, clean, and organic.

> A few to mention are by Dr. Bronners, Weleda, and Young Living, which are all of great quality and purity (from seed to seal).

Forging Ahead and Inner House Cleaning

During that time of change, it was important to ensure that I no longer unintentionally added any chemicals to my body. Simply walking around in our world today exposes us to more poisons than we realize. So whatever was in my control, I wanted to control, and within a short period of time, I was making healthier and more conscious decisions about what went into and onto my body. Somehow, my body actually felt the difference from these clean products, and it felt as though my body was thanking me. My mood was better, and I felt lighter, the more I used organic, non-toxic products.

It is much easier to find clean products nowadays, and a good place to begin is at a local health food store or supermarket, such as Whole Foods, Fairway Organics, Trader Joe's, and Henry's. Browsing the Web will bring up a good number of websites where you can easily find what you are looking for.

So basically, you have to make sure that the labels state that the products are free of chemicals such as parabens, laurel sodium sulfate, propylene glycol, phthalates, and any synthetics. Ingredients like parabens are cancer-causing and affect the hormones of men and women. Sodium lauryl sulfate and ammonium laureth sulfate are also seriously harmful. According to the *Journal of the American College of Toxicology*, they can cause cancer, fatalities, eye damage, liver and kidney damage, and depression, to name a few of the side-effects. [1] Because of my background in research, I had a strong urge to investigate until I reached a point where I felt I had read enough to make better-informed decisions about what I was purchasing to put in and on my body.

As for the cost, as I did more research I slowly came to understand that these products cost more for a few reasons—and that I really align with these reasons. Many of the organic companies operate with a vision that includes providing products that improve the quality of our lives and the health of our planet. When something is produced organically, the process is more involved, which results in higher labor costs. And since many organic companies are small, they aren't able to offer products at a "competitive" price. Like with most things—if you want quality, you usually have to pay for it. What I didn't anticipate was the savings I enjoyed after being on these products for a few years. I had virtually no medical bills and lower health insurance premiums due to a healthier state of being. My suggestion is to weigh the long-term benefits and cost savings when comparing the cost of using more wholesome and vital products.

---

[1] "Final Report on the Safety Assessment of Sodium Lauryl Sulfate," *Journal of the American College of Toxicology*, 2,. no. 7 (1983),. p. 23.

At the same time, I had to make sure that whatever I ingested was also organic, at least to the best of my ability. When I say organic, I mean the "real" organic, which is labeled as "USDA Organic." This means it is 100 percent organic and pure, as far as the government can certify it, with no pesticides, herbicides, fungicides, genetically modified ingredients, hormones, or anything else that will harm you. All else is junk. Don't go for the simply "certified organic" or "all natural" labels. These labels are misleading and many foods labeled this way contain a large percentage of harmful ingredients, which can actually negate the positive benefits contained in the remaining organic ingredients.

That's not to say that you should avoid local farmers whom you know personally. He or she may not be organically certified, but his farming methods may produce food that is healthful and organic. For example, I have a garden. And although it's not USDA certified organic, it does not get any more organic than my garden! I actually go beyond the government certification requirements, because my seeds are organic and my soil has been organic for at least five years. In addition to fruits and vegetables, we also purchase pasture-raised organic meats and eggs from a farmer we know and trust.

I mention this because it is important to understand and share information in order to live a healthy lifestyle. Reports show that ingesting harmful, non-organic food leads to many diseases that are directly related to pesticide, herbicide, and fungicide exposure. Thanks to current research, it is now pretty well known that the chemicals found in pesticides alter our hormone levels to the extreme of making us sterile in less than two generations, as well as altering our genetic makeup, not to mention causing health issues like birth defects, serious diseases such as cancer, neurological problems, and many other problems (according to the EPA). Please refer to the Resource section in back of the book for the details.

In my case, as I was addressing these issues, my goal was to conceive. I wasn't fighting a debilitating disease, and so my main focus was to maintain a healthy body, primarily a healthy reproductive system. After a year of eating organically and from natural sources, I began a mild detoxification program using a greens drink known as Greens First, which contains 10-plus servings of fruits and vegetables in every serving (and is the best tasting greens drink on the market, in my opinion).

Eventually, my husband and I began enjoying this clean, flavorful food, along with other whole food supplements, and again, we felt the difference in our bodies soon enough. Our digestion began to improve dramatically, my skin cleared up, my menstrual cycle was becoming more regular, our sleep improved, and there were many more benefits as well. We began a supplementation routine that our acupuncturist-nutritionist recommended, with whole food, organic, and wonderful products known as Standard Process. This is a whole food supplement

> About Greens First: For most people, it is nearly impossible to get 10 servings of fruits and vegetables in what we eat daily, and so this stuff was perfect. Also, these vegetables are flash-dried to retain the natural enzymes of fresh raw juice. The cracked cell wall chlorella is digestible and aids in detoxifying metals and other toxins, which enter our bodies each and every day. Overall, this yummy drink boosts my immune system and when my immunity is strong, then my body is naturally in a healthier and stronger state.

company that practices integrity during the whole process, from the seed to the supplement. Their products are available primarily through health practitioners. As you read their labels, you see there is nothing synthetic or manufactured about them; their goal is to provide whole food ingredients that have all the nutrients contained in the food or plant. And to me, that makes this company awesome, and after many years, my family and I (including my extended family) still take their supplements daily.

If possible, I suggest finding a health care professional who can guide you through the best options for your optimal health. A nutritionist, an acupuncturist, a

> Other great sources of clean supplements are Emerson Ecologics, Thorne Research, Young Living, and Nordic Naturals.

holistic doctor, a naturopath, and sometimes even a holistic chiropractor can get you started. If you would like to begin on your own, without a medical professional to guide you when introducing a new modality into your lifestyle, attend group meetings like those held by Young Living, where you're able to gain much information and support from the community. Whatever route you choose, simply take the first step and go on from there at your own pace.

Since I was eager to conceive, I dove right in with Michael, my acupuncturist, and eventually I became my own expert. I was told that I actually had a toxic liver. Well, I knew I needed a clean liver and purified kidneys, so I made sure to keep my acupuncture appointments. After a number of treatments I had a liver that could adequately eliminate daily toxins, and kidneys that were healthy enough to ensure proper filtering of my blood.

As an aside, during these various visits, my acupuncturist also ruled out the possibility of other problems, such as a thyroid condition, by performing various forms of alternative testing—and no surprise to me, everything else was normal, just as the fertility specialist had said. While maintaining my health, my husband and I also made sure to keep trying to conceive, just in case.

Stress Can Be a Hold Up

When we were about to take the final step to detoxify my body from all that had accumulated in me during my lifetime, I realized that I was very stressed out, and that this would not support our attempts at baby making. Of course many people are stressed out, and there are many ways to deal with stress. Something that I did, was to remind myself to just do my best and to make time to relax at some point during my day or week. When responsibilities grew to be too overwhelming, I simply took a little break, either for a day, a weekend, long weekend, or even a month—whatever my gut was telling me I needed in order to keep going without burning out.

I began researching how stress can affect baby making, and realized that it's a large contributing factor to infertility. Basically, studies show that if someone is under stress for prolonged periods of time, the adrenaline produced during these "flight-or-flight" times can affect the hormone levels, ovulation, and can even compromise the immune system. This leaves the body with very little of the energy required for baby making.

My best bet was to try any sort of stress reduction technique in collaboration with what my health professional was suggesting. Here is what I did, and what I sometimes suggest to anyone who is having trouble conceiving. I continued releasing stress at the gym, did yoga, went for long walks in local parks, and sometimes even enjoyed a nap by a lake at a nearby park. I enjoyed bike riding, hiking, vacations, and lots of time with friends. Occasionally, I would read or meditate, although meditation really became a part of my life after I gave birth.

Nowadays, in addition to the above and meditating, I also find peace in chanting, writing, and grounding myself during times of need through visualization techniques. And don't forget spending quality, loving time with your partner! The stronger the feeling of love is between the two partners, the better the chances of creating the space for a baby.

How Healthy Is "All Natural"?

So back to my acupuncturist's plan. My acupuncturist made sure that he was ridding my physical vessel of the toxic buildup it had bio-accumulated. Don't get me wrong, I grew up eating wonderful home-cooked Mediterranean meals, and I virtually had no idea what most fast food tasted like. It was not until college that I began to eat carelessly, and honor my body less for various reasons—mostly due to an overloaded day, which included a full-time job, an additional part-time job, and full-time college schedule. I ate whatever was cheap and quick. Without realizing it, I had welcomed the nutrient-deficient Western American diet into my life. And my body, and baby making, were paying the price.

That was for a just for a few years though, and then as I mentioned earlier, I began to take care of myself again through various forms of physical activity, and a so-called "healthy diet." What I didn't know was that due to the lack of the right information, I was actually poisoning myself in a very subtle way, meaning that I didn't really know what was in the food and supplements I was consuming. They seemed healthy and natural, but I didn't realize how synthetic and unnatural most of the ingredients I consumed were. A documentary like *Food Inc.* can get someone interested enough to look into exactly what they are consuming. I am still learning about the healthiest way to eat.

And so, with much gratitude to my acupuncturist, I was slowly getting rid of the "unhealthy" within me, and replacing it with the "healthy." This gradual healthy replacement in my body was probably my best option at that time. Why it's best to flush out toxins gradually was explained to me during a health workshop, where a quote from a very well-known chiropractor was shared: "If you give an organic banana to a toxic person, they can have an adverse reaction. It's best to ease their body into a healthier state, by slowly replacing the toxins with healing substitutes." And so a nice slow detoxification and cleansing was my route for a while. If you are thinking about detoxing, for ideal results I suggest doing it with the help of a health practitioner or getting a good amount of information about the process. Under the right circumstances, this can truly be a surprisingly pleasant experience.

My Detoxification Goes Deeper

After going through several detoxes, I now am aware of how sacred and spiritual a detox can be. Various forms of detoxes and fasts have actually been associated with religious and spiritual practices from the beginning of time. This is a practice that unites your body, mind and soul and aligns you with the Creator. If you're trying to conceive, I would suggest cleansing or detoxifying first. Not only does it create a healthy body so that you are able to conceive faster, it also provides a wonderful physical environment for your baby once you are pregnant. I now personally know of many friends that will intentionally detox before they attempt to conceive. Many attest that they were pregnant within a few months after a proper, healthy detox. I can vouch for the same.

At this time in our lives, my husband and I enjoy the benefits of an annual detoxification program put out by Standard Process, known as their 21-day purification cleanse, which involves eating only specific fruits and vegetables, preferably raw, or steamed for just a minute or two, along with certain whole food supplements that aid in cleansing your important body organs. I cannot imagine my life without the annual experience of this cleansing program. During this detox, we honor the process, respecting what we are experiencing on a physical level. We try to stay away from media in order to eliminate the delusional dark emotions they are evoking, such as fear. We also meditate and pray in order to connect, stay attuned to, and receive clear visions and messages as our bodies' vibrations seem to be elevated by not being weighed down by toxins. And during this time, we make sure to enjoy a treatment of acupuncture, colon hydrotherapy, Reiki, raindrop technique, massage, chiropractic adjustments, and basically anything that assists in eliminating the waste better, faster and more effectively. Through this detox, we cleanse our liver, kidneys, colon and bladder, as these are what will primarily keep our bodies healthy, harmonious and humming. During our cleanse, we have experienced feelings of euphoria, transcendence, clarity, simplicity, gratitude, and a stronger sense of faith and understanding.

The first few days of the cleanse are always rough, but once over that hurdle, you will immediately begin to feel better. If you feel that you are already living a healthy lifestyle, and are considering inviting another child into your family, as I've said, I encourage you to detox prior to starting to conceive. This way your child will enter a very wholistically healthy environment from the very beginning.

Meditation

Take a few deep breaths, relax your body and count backwards from 10. As you deepen your relaxation and various thoughts begin to enter your mind, simply acknowledge them and return back to a still state. Imagine a bright golden yellow sun directly above your body, shining and showering its golden light all around and throughout your body. Picture all parts of yourself being showered by this light. Tell yourself you are perfectly healthy and you honor yourself and your body, that all is well in your world and your health is perfect. When you feel complete with this vision, slowly begin coming back, and eventually open your eyes. You may continue by affirming throughout your day that you are "perfectly healthy."

Grounding Visualization for Stress Reduction:

Close your eyes, take 10 deep intentional breaths. First fill your belly with air, then your chest, and release the air from your belly first and then your chest. As you release the air, you are exhaling from your mouth. Slowly visualize yourself in a forest. See the forest. See yourself entering a large tree, like a redwood tree. Be in the tree. Feel the bottom of your feet growing roots that slowly extend all the way down to the core of the Earth. You are releasing your stress down through your feet, your roots and into the center of the Earth. Then, slowly see a pulse of energy pump up from the core to your roots, up through your feet, your spine and up to your head. See a few pumps of energy come up to you. Re-energize, re-boot, thank the tree, the forest and Mother Earth. Open your eyes. You are now grounded. This is a good way to start your day and end your day. You can use it as needed throughout the day as well.

CHAPTER 3

Conception

After all that work trying for three years to conceive, we began exploring other options for expanding our family. We had agreed that if we weren't pregnant within the year, we would embrace adoption. I was so stressed out, between a busy career and this whole fertility experience, that we felt it might be time to let go of the whole natural conception route. So, after all my gradual hard-core cleansing, and the subtle yet drastic changes in our lives, my husband and I decided we were going on a one-month vacation to Europe.

Before I left, I visited my acupuncturist, and he said he believed that I was now ready to conceive, and a relaxing vacation would be perfect—the missing ingredient. He gave me about 20 different types of supplements to take with me, and asked me to be sure not miss even one dose. So off to vacation I went, and for the first week I was alone in Greece with my parents for some good quality family catch up.

My Invitation to My Son

My mother suggested we take a boat ride to a nearby Greek island that is known worldwide for the Church of the Virgin Mary. People visit this church from all parts of the world asking and praying for miracles. As I entered this sacred space, there was no denying its healing energy. I felt ensconced by it. I knew it was time to ask for help in becoming a mother, and that this was the perfect place to ask. And so I went and prayed, and I added to my prayer that I was ready for our child to join us. I could feel my prayer being heard.

Because of the experience I had in that church, I have come to believe that when inviting, conceiving, and raising a child, the spiritual nurturing is just as important as the physical. It is crucial to be mindful of the interconnected triad of mind, body and soul. One component cannot fully be there without the other, as all three are what make us the beings that we are. And so when my body was ready to receive and conceive our child, it was important that I communicated with our Source and invited my child into our life. This was the first direct spiritual connection I had with my child. Somehow I knew with certainty that the Virgin Mary had heard my prayer and communication, and that my child knew it was time. I felt a sort of peace come over me about the whole fertility challenge, like I knew it was over. I can't really articulate this feeling, but all I can say is that there was a "knowing" that now I could have my child.

Conceiving

The next week my husband joined us, and we traveled to another island for some fun. I had completely forgotten which days I was ovulating, I didn't take my temperature to find out if it was right for baby making, because I had forgotten my thermometer at home. I made sure to take my supplements every day, though. We had an amazing time, and two weeks later, we flew to Paris.

A few days into our trip to Paris, I was lying in bed, and had a euphoric feeling pass over me. For whatever reason, I simply knew we had conceived. I mentioned it to my husband, and we decided not to pay it any mind, and just have a good time. We traveled through the south of France, and experienced one of the most unforgettable trips.

On my flight home, I had cramps. When my sister-in-law picked me up, she revealed to me that she had had a dream that I was pregnant, and I explained that I had been having a different sort of cramping that day. A few days after we settled back in at home, I just had to check, and I took a pregnancy test at 5:00 a.m. *It was positive!* I ran to tell my sleeping husband, who replied "Cool…" and went back to sleep. When he woke up, he ran to ask me if that was real or a dream he had. In an ecstatic manner I told him that we were pregnant, and then he lost his mind from joy. We were like little children who just received the biggest Christmas present that ever existed. And no, I am not psychic, but two weeks into my pregnancy, I just knew our baby was here to stay, and that it was a boy. I was so sure, that I began telling everyone that we were having a boy—and I was only a few weeks along!

The Importance of the Process

Shortly after we conceived, I soon came to realize how important it is for me to remind myself to trust the process, and how events unfold in my life. I was grateful that my son had us wait for him. Our world today is much more toxic than when I was a child, and it is my belief that most of the health issues that children have when they enter this world today are due to this overwhelming toxicity, resulting in all the allergies, learning disabilities, diseases, and disorders. Today's children are trying to tell us something about the world we live in. And if my son had chosen to be one of these canaries in the coal mine, he would have probably joined us much earlier with some sort of health issue for sure. But I do think that his soul chose this path for whatever reason, and made sure that his mother and father cleaned up really well before he got here. And we are thankful to him for the awareness he brought us, which led to the life that we lead today.

I always say that our children guide us as much as we guide them. As my son taught me how I can honor my body, and my daughter helped me believe that I can tap into my soul and spiritual side again with great outcomes. And she did this from the womb as well. This journey and lifestyle are the flowers that blossomed from the seeds my children planted when they became part of our world. This book is a part of this magnificent flower garden.

Meditation

Close your eyes, take a few long deep breaths and relax. Imagine your child in a little garden. See yourself walking towards him or her and picture yourself talking to your child. Tell your child that you love her and that you are now ready for her to join you. For a little bit, picture yourself hugging, playing, laughing, or anything else that comes naturally to you. Before you go, say that you'd like to see your child soon for some more of what you just experienced together.

After you practice this a few times, you can also try envisioning your uterus as a healthy, sacred, and wonderful place for your child to enter. See it bathed with golden light or blue light, if you feel that it needs a little help or healing. Know and affirm that all is well and perfectly suited for you and your child to begin your journey together.

CHAPTER 4

Healthy Pregnancy

I believe that our role as wholistic parents begins at the very magical moment that our universe decides to join egg and sperm to create a life here on earth. The instant that special union takes place in her womb, a mother's body provides health and sustenance to her unborn child. Experts agree that during the first nine months of a baby's life, children experience more growth and development than any other time in their existence. So doesn't it make sense for an expecting mother to begin consciously nurturing her unborn child from the moment of conception?

This is the first step of what I call wholistic parenting. And by "w"holistic, I mean, honoring the triad of the mind, body, and spirit of the unborn child and nurturing him or her in the healthiest way possible from the moment of conception.

Life Slowly Begins to Change Even More

Once our child entered our realm, I immediately called the obstetrician and scheduled my very first prenatal visit—the eight-week-pregnant appointment. When I arrived at the doctor's office, I waited the usual two hours, was finally seen, and went through the typical routine of blood and urine tests, and a sonogram. My husband and I were thrilled (except for the two-hour waiting part). And hooray, of course we were pregnant! So, we were given the mega-sized prenatal vitamins, and then scheduled to return for regular monthly visits, including a sonogram and all the other unnecessary exams.

Here I was, barely pregnant with my little one on the way, and living a whole new lifestyle. And so I did a reality check! First, I embraced how I was now sharing my body with a whole other being. Can I say anything that adequately explains how mysterious and wondrous this time is for an expecting mother? I was no longer responsible for myself alone, but for a whole other human being, who was entirely dependent on me. It became very clear that I needed to make responsible choices and be very conscious of what both my unborn child and I were exposed to.

Upon my first prenatal visit to my acupuncturist, I announced my great news and thanked him for all his guidance. Within the first few minutes of that visit, he told me to throw the prenatal vitamins the doctor had given me into the garbage. This is where he thought they belonged. He elaborated on how they do not provide anything "real" and beneficial to the baby. None of the vitamins or minerals in the capsules were derived from nature—they were completely synthetic. He proceeded to give me supplements by Standard Process known as their "prenatal formula of supplements." Not only were these supplements organic, but they also provided bioavailable ingredients that both bodies (mine and the baby's) could actually absorb and make use of, as opposed to the prenatals provided by my obstetrician. I used this organic supplement protocol during both of my pregnancies. I also made sure to receive acupuncture treatments and chiropractic adjustments once a week to keep my body's energy flowing healthfully and my spine in alignment as much as possible. It was imperative for my body's energy to be serving my pregnancy and my baby, instead of a possible ailment. *Note: Some acupuncture treatments are not safe for pregnant women. Let your acupuncturist know if you are trying to conceive and as soon as you suspect you are pregnant, so he or she can treat you appropriately.*

Exercise During Pregnancy

During both of my pregnancies, I made sure to exercise for as many weeks as I could. Not only was it necessary for me to release my pent-up stress and emotions, it was also physically healthy for my body and for my baby's. And of course I kept my spiritual side maintained as well by keeping up with my yoga classes, walking, writing, and doing a bit of meditation. Honestly, these simple little steps lead to a very happy, healthy, and fulfilling pregnancy. I never had any nausea, discomfort, complication, or any sort of uncomfortable feelings during my pregnancies. Although it may seem virtually impossible once your baby arrives to keep these activities in the mix, but as soon as you can get back into them again, the better it will be for you and your entire family.

I made sure to lighten my workouts by tweaking them so that I was no longer doing hard-core step aerobics and weight lifting. Instead, I would go on the step master and the treadmill. I even biked in the gym and outdoors for as long as I was comfortable. I would feel completely energized, as well as mentally and emotionally clear after my workouts. It was exhilarating. I know of mothers who enjoyed Pilates up until their delivery date! I would be physically active once or twice a week, and I reserved one day a week for yoga. This combination simply made life easier—there is no denying that. It also allowed for a physically comfortable and healthy pregnancy. Furthermore, I believe the beginning stages of my labor for both children were manageable because of my workouts, yoga, meditations, chiropractic care, acupuncture, diet, right supplementation—basically the entire wholistic lifestyle.

> In the *Huffington Post* article by by Caroline Gregoire posted on December 3, 2013, she writes, "Research has found that the health benefits of prenatal yoga are many, from a decreased risk of prenatal depression to improved sleep to decreased back pain and nausea, according to the Mayo Clinic. A 2012 study also found that prenatal yoga could help to prevent complications during pregnancy. The research, published in the medical journal *Preventive Medicine*, showed that pregnant women who practiced yoga for one hour, three times per week, were less likely to have low birth weight babies, pregnancy-related diabetes and high blood pressure."

Integrative Approach to Pregnancy

A few months into my first pregnancy, once the great news had fully spread, friends gifted me with several best-selling, mainstream books on pregnancy, which I simply felt no connection to. So in addition to obtaining information and articles from my acupuncturist, I also began researching on the Internet in order to understand what exactly was taking place in my body as well my child's. I quickly learned that it would be best for me to continue my organic diet and minimize my exposure to toxins, such as plastics. I'm grateful for the studies I read about how much BPA and related toxins were found today inside umbilical cords—and leaking into our unborn children's systems. (See resources section for a few of these studies).

Another factor I knew I wanted to pay attention to and manage was my stress level. I was dealing with a very challenging time in my personal family life, as well as my career. I had a feeling that I would need to be creative, if I was going to keep my stress levels low throughout my pregnancy. Thankfully, my best friend gave us the perfect Christmas gift and suggestion, which was a pack of spiritual DVDs. So, on New Year's Eve 2006, my husband and I watched spiritually-motivated DVDs and read sections from various spiritual books.

That night we were inspired by all the insight that had shined on us. This led us to enjoy several newly self-created projects, such as drawing happy pictures on my belly, writing out words on it such as "Happy, Healthy and Perfect," and keeping these on my body as long as the eyeliner lasted. Why perform such acts, you ask? Well, back on that New Years Eve we viewed a DVD with excerpts from Dr. Masaru Emoto's book *Messages in Water*, and we were intrigued by his findings about how water was beautifully affected by prayer, music, and good words, and how interestingly the opposite was true in response to any sort of negativity. And so for us it only made sense to do all this, since not only are we mostly made of water, but our baby was surrounded by, lived in, and was developing in water in my womb.

We also relaxed during meditations, said and wrote our affirmations, and basically relished a husband and wife bond that grew stronger and stronger by the day. My baby and I enjoyed moments of Native American flute music at night. My husband would also read to my belly a few nights a week, while the little guy inside tumbled all around.

One thing I also discovered was that whenever I would get angry or stressed out, I would sing a song—usually the ABC song, and my son would go from kicking and turning to complete stillness. I believe it sent him the message that everything was okay. I urge every expecting mother to sing to her belly. Music has been known throughout time as a form of relaxation and healing.

As a mother sings, she relaxes and so does her baby. It can also be considered as a moment of bonding between a mother and child, as she sings and her baby responds. This is something sweet that anyone can enjoy and even have fun with, so I say stretch those vocal cords and sing away, mamas. This is something we have been doing forever, throughout every culture. Let us not forget how beautiful it can be.

Pre- and Peri-Natal Psychology

You can see how important it was to me that I enjoyed my pregnancy, my connection to my husband and to my unborn child. It was also important to me to stay as positive and optimistic as I could during my pregnancy. I had read about the significance of a mother's state of mind during pregnancy, and there is actually a vast amount of research showing that a mother's state of mind during pregnancy can affect her child more than genetics ever could. More specifically, the whole idea about how important it is to be conscious of your well being prior to childbirth is called pre- and peri-natal psychology. This is where parents tune in to their emotional well being prior to parenthood.

Dr. Thomas R. Verny is a researcher who explored this field extensively. He has written many books and hosts workshops and lectures around the world on how the quality of our heart energy (physically, emotionally and spiritually) during pregnancy impacts the developing baby's experience and entire life. Many of his studies, cited in his blog and book, *The Secret Life of the Unborn Child*, draw "correlations between a state of health in adulthood, adolescence, or childhood, and what happened when the mother was pregnant... In terms of public health, it appears today that nothing is more important than the health and well being of pregnant women. In terms of research, nothing is more important than to study the factors influencing fetal growth and fetal development."[2]

---

[2]   http://www.wombecology.com,

Dr. Verny found that when a mother both consciously and subconsciously wanted to be pregnant and had invited her baby in to her life, the child thrived in the womb. However, when the mother neither consciously nor subconsciously wanted the baby, the child would feel the effects of its mother's hostile emotional environment. During one of his workshops, Dr. Verny discussed the research of an Italian colleague who explored how an unborn child was impacted by its mother's conscious and subconscious feelings about the pregnancy. During this study, the Italian doctor was actually informed by the mother that not only did she not want her child, but also resented the intrusive presence she felt in her body. During an ultrasound, the doctor looked at the baby while the mother expressed her feelings of resentment of him and about her pregnancy. The doctor noticed that the baby reacted by curling up into a tiny ball in a corner of its mother's uterus. It looked as if he was trying to make himself very small. This study shows how even in utero, a baby can sense the power of the mother's heart or feelings—and be affected by them.

According to Dr. Verny's lifelong studies, Joseph Chilton Pearce's research, Dr. Andrew Newberg's data, and large amounts of readily available information, everything that the mother feels is directly communicated to her baby. This shapes the architecture of the child's brain and ultimately the life she or he will lead later on (not to mention our world community). If many of us choose to consciously parent in a positive way during pregnancy, we will ultimately be changing our world as we know it by supporting the souls that we invite into it.

Natural Child Birth Classes

Speaking of inviting my child into this world, I knew I would need an initial tool to help eliminate any fears that would come up for me about labor. I began to look into the best way to experience my first labor and delivery. I wanted to increase the chances of providing my baby with a positive and healthy entrance into our world. It just so happened that during another one of our very long and draining visits at my ob/gyn's, I noticed an advertisement for Lamaze classes. I embarked on some Internet research and stumbled upon ads for the Bradley Method classes instead.

Somehow these just felt like a better option for me. I now recommend the Bradley Method classes to expecting mothers both for the bond it creates

between mother, father, and unborn child, and also for the educational aspect. Although I was learning a lot just by reading, taking this class helped me to believe in myself, and empowered me to take my delivery into my own hands. (No pun intended.)

There was a whole other aspect to giving birth that included hospital administration and policy, legalities and liabilities, and so forth. Ultimately, these classes opened my eyes to how much money was behind the entire birthing process. What else is new, and why did I have greater expectations? Once again, my husband and I had to do our own legwork in order to make informed and conscious decisions. This decision is highly personal, so I suggest strongly that you do not simply put all your faith in one person or system.

First Hard Lesson Learned

I remember being misguided by the system and my ob/gyn, and it was a lesson that changed me forever. When I reached my fifth month of pregnancy, I was instructed to take the triple test to make sure that our

Mother's Intuition Grows Louder

With the Bradley Method, I learned to listen to my body, instead of medical personnel and the red tape involved in child birthing. What followed next was listening to what felt right to me. My intuition was beginning to kick up in volume. For centuries, cultures have honored a woman's ability to listen and receive guidance from within. Many cultures have different practices and rituals with which they connect with their unborn child. In Africa, ancient cultures like the Dagara practice rituals which create direct contact between the unborn child and expert shamans, while the child is in his mother's belly. They ask the unborn child what its purpose here on Earth will be, and what the child will offer to its community and humanity. Nowadays, our modern medical, high tech society has disregarded the validity of our intuition and the important role it plays in the connection between mother and child. As a result, we all turn to outside support and guidance. Never doubt your internal voice! If you're seeking the answer *out there*, you risk being misguided and possibly even losing your way.

baby was healthy and did not have any genetic abnormalities. This is a blood test that looks into three substances in your blood that assess possibilities of genetic disorders. What I learned later was that this is a very flawed, not to mention unnecessary, exam that often results in a false positive. In this case, a false positive means that the test results indicate the possibility that the child will be born with Down's syndrome (or another disorder). The test requires verification with an amniocentesis, which analyzes the DNA from the amniotic fluid. And this is what happened to us.

After a long, three-way conversation with the doctor, which instilled so much doubt and fear in us, my husband and I decided to go through with it—even though there was a risk that the amniocentesis could result in my losing my child. Wow. Until this day, I cannot tell you why I decided to go ahead with it. I knew at such a deep, intuitive level that my baby was very healthy. After the exam, I sensed that my child and his sacred space felt invaded. Normally my baby was very active, day and night. And for the very first time in my pregnancy there was a sudden, eerie quiet in my belly—and it lasted for three long days. I remember wishing and longing that he would move. I just wanted to know that he was okay. Although I knew it was important to remain positive, I allowed myself to cry and experience my emotions during this time, because I regretted not following my intuition.

That was my first parenting lesson: Always listen to your inner guidance, no matter what is being thrown your way. It is the only thing you can be sure of. I was disappointed in myself, not to mention that my baby's quietness was unnerving. So my husband and I decided to write all over my belly, take videos, draw silly faces and beautiful words, sing, and just cheer the three of us up. It was great.

When it was time for the test results, I found out that my ob/gyn's very reputable busy office lost my results, and I had to wait two more days. At this point, though, I no longer needed the test to tell me that my baby was perfectly healthy. Of course, all was well, but again this was another sign we should have paid attention to. If a medical doctor is instilling fear in a new parent in order to guide their decision, I think it is an indication that his advice is not guided by the heart. If this happens to you, head for the hills!

I am fortunate that I did not suffer any negative consequences as a result of the amniocentesis. But had it gone any other way, I could have been another mom who simply "felt and knew" all was healthy with her child, but just didn't trust herself enough to make her own decision about having the test or not. To often stories are shared where a mother intuitively knew whether or not to do something, but didn't follow her gut, only to suffer a lifetime consequence. I now am aware that no one knows better than me. What my gut is telling me *can* be trusted—and this belief has never failed me since that incident.

I made sure that nothing like this occurred while I was pregnant with my daughter (my second child). When it came to how my pregnancy was handled with her, I was aligned, confident, and assertive when I needed to be. When in doubt, tune in. Your answer is already there and is waiting to be heard. If you need support for the answer, then seek it out from the right people and resources so that you can make a decision without ambivalence. And if all is great and there are no major decisions to be made during your pregnancy, then simply make sure you are in a healthy place wholistically.

Meditation:

Helpful meditation for a heated or stressful moment during pregnancy:

1. *Take a very long deep breath in, followed by a long exhale. Remove yourself from the stressful situation and repeat the breathing.*
2. *Place one hand on your heart and one on your belly. Picture your baby; picture yourself holding him or her safely and lovingly.*
3. *Then, picture yourself being held safely and lovingly by a warm, golden light. Take a few more deep breaths while holding this vision.*

This will allow you to connect from the heart for the benefit of your child as well as yourself. If you wish to return to the same situation or environment, try again with a different approach, otherwise remove yourself from the situation, and approach the issue another day.

Meditation during pregnancy:

1. *Dim or turn off the lights, light a candle, and lay down.*
2. *Rub your belly a few times. Take a few deep breaths and relax.*
3. *Begin to see yourself playing with your child under the golden light of the sun.*
4. *Notice your child in a happy and thriving state. See the landscape, feel the warmth shining all over the two of you. You are protected, you are safe, and all is well in your world. Enjoy your time together.*
5. *Tell your child you will be back again soon for some more play time.*
6. *When you are done, open your eyes.*

You can enjoy this meditation during a nice warm bath, or in bed after a long, challenging day.

CHAPTER 5

Who's Delivering My Baby?

While I was growing more and more confident as a preg-o, the Bradley classes also fueled and empowered us in some new decision making. During our Bradley classes, my husband and I realized that we could actually enjoy most of the delivery process, which I admit I was initially so nervous about. I had read books that even talked about orgasmic birthing experiences, where mothers actually worked so well with their bodies that once their baby was entering the world, mommy was climaxing from the joy she was experiencing in her entire being. Were they serious? I had to read a few more of those stories before I could actually believe this to be true.

We understood that there was normally no need to rush to a hospital when labor begins, and much of the work can be done at home, whether it's just between mom and dad, or with the extra help of a doula. We learned about what signs to look for in order to understand which of the three stages of labor we were in, and to recognize when it was time to go to the hospital.

We were introduced to birthing plans, birthing center options, and the differences between midwives and ob/gyns. And there is even a difference between a *medwife,* as they are commonly referred to, and a midwife, since there are varying degrees of natural birth midwives.

Medwives typically practice in an ob/gyn's office, are certified nurse midwives, or have a nursing degree. Medwives follow hospital protocol, use technology more often, and sometimes may even have less of a spiritual connection with their patient.

We learned about home births and many more options. We were grateful to our Bradley instructor for all that she helped us with. We also had the opportunity to decide on how we planned to invite our little baby into this world.

Once my husband and I began envisioning a beautiful, spiritual, calm delivery day, we suddenly realized that our ob/gyn might not agree with even one-quarter of what we had in mind. So we brought our birthing plan to him during my 32-week appointment. When we handed him our plan, without really even reading it, he immediately began a fear tactic by replying, "Sure. We can make all the birth plans you want. But if your child comes out with a life-long debilitating illness as a result of all this, it's usually the doctor that gets all the blame—and I plan on keeping my house." After our initial shock, my husband and I just said "Thank you," walked out of the room, and never looked back.

Now, at the tail-end of my pregnancy, we were on the hunt for a midwife. We quickly found a medwife instead, and it was an improvement, not to mention a step in the direction we knew we were heading. She was part of a medical practice and at the time, we felt comfortable with the idea of her having an ob/gyn in her office to back her up in case anything came up. Our feelings and insecurities were due to a lack of information about what is truly needed during delivery. I can now say that all the information we had gained was just an introduction. For my daughter, we had a midwife who was affiliated with one of the best labor and delivery hospital units, very well known for its natural birthing center, at St. Luke's Roosevelt Hospital in New York City.

Home or Hospital?

When I am asked about birthing, I usually respond by asking my friends to first begin thinking about where they plan on delivering, and allow for their own educated decisions. Home or the hospital? If you decide on a hospital, I would first pick which hospital allows for parents to participate in the delivery process. St. Luke's, for example, does not get involved with their Birthing Center at all, unless they are instructed to intervene by your midwife, ob/gyn, or delivery team. The expecting parents enjoy a home-like environment, a spa-sized jacuzzi tub, freedom to walk around and try new, comfortable positions during labor, or hang from a swing—you get the idea. And so once you research, visit, and decide on a birth location, you can then contact the hospital and ask them for a list of their affiliated ob/gyns or midwives. I personally asked who they recommend from their list. And from there, you can begin interviewing birthing professionals until you meet the person best qualified to help you deliver your child.

We picked great hospitals for both children to be delivered in. (But, if I were to ever have a third, it would be a home birth.) We made sure that we had the option of a bath, shower or hot tub, and no IV to hold me down. This way we could experience walking around as much as possible without being strapped to a bed, no mandatory vaccinations, no formula feeding, the baby could remain with mom at all times, there were great rooms, and basically an environment where our midwife was trusted so that she could do her job without much administrative interference. For our first birth, we decided on no epidural, no induction, basically nothing more than delivering a child as nature intended.

The fact that we have one of the highest birth mortality rates of the industrialized world would not entice me to give birth in a hospital. It would encourage me to look at other options. Knowing that the hospital's concerns about liability and political interests are of much greater importance to them than my baby and me is very discomforting, to say the least. The hospital administration and staff do not know you,

I encourage every expecting mother to at least look into enjoying a home birth. Believe me when I tell you that when you hear another mother share her beautiful experiences about her home birth, you may suddenly have an inner calling to want to do the same for yourself, your baby, and your family. I know mothers who have had vaginal births after caesarean (VBACs) at home, as well as breech births. I now believe that virtually any kind of birth is safer at home than in a hospital. Of course, many concerns arise once we hear this inner calling that are merely doubts trying to cloud our inner voice once again. These arise from misinformation we have "heard" or read somewhere about home births. And once again, education on this matter is the path to a clear, confident decision about home birthing.

most don't care much to know you, and will never see you again aside from your brief time with them while you trust them to deliver your baby. You have no personal connection with them, and they have none with your child. Their priorities and goals are usually different than yours. And let's not hide the fact that they may even consider you to be a nuisance as you begin to express your intention to have a memorable, beautiful, spiritual connection with your child while it is entering our world.

What better place than the comfort of your own home, your own props, essential oils, your candles, your music, your own bed and bathroom... your own team. With a home birth, you create the world your child will come into. You don't have to worry about bright lights, strangers poking you or taking your child away from you, an extraneous authority undermining you—possibly belittling you—or any of the feelings that many of us mothers have experienced in a hospital, even if we bring our own wonderful entourage with us to this facility.

The Ancient Practice of Midwifery

There is a limit as to what you can do if you are delivering in a hospital. So why not consider staying home with a midwife? And if you are concerned about anything going wrong at home, just know that midwifery is an ancient practice and midwives have been delivering babies far longer than doctors. Their philosophies and restrictions are not comparable. For example, today it is much easier to find a midwife to deliver a breeched baby than an obstetrician. Most obstetricians do not want to take the risk of a lawsuit, and would likely perform a caesarean, whereas a midwife is more likely to do what she can to turn the baby or even to deliver the baby vaginally in the breeched position. And many midwives now bring their own equipment, such as baby monitors, to your home. It is well worth your time to look into home birthing, and into finding a midwife who will suit your needs and answer all your questions and concerns, regardless of where you plan to birth.

Bluntly stated, in my opinion the modern medical field has nothing to offer when compared to midwifery—especially when birthing naturally. It couldn't compete if it tried. And when I say this I mean that a modern obstetrician cannot (and will not) do many of the tasks needed for delivery that a truly experienced midwife can. As I mentioned, a modern obstetrician most likely will not deliver a breeched baby, whereas a midwife has been trained to deliver babies in the breeched or posterior positions. A midwife can also allow for the option of beautiful water births, perineal massage so that you do not tear, meditations, labor positioning, home births, nursing, hypnotic birthing, and so much more. The reason for this is that midwifery is a sacred practice, which women and children have depended on pretty much from the beginning of assisted birthing. The modern medical field jumped in on birthing fairly recently for various reasons. And so a doctor's knowledge and experience is limited, not to mention often disconnected from the actual birthing process itself.

How many obstetricians have versatility like that of a midwife? Few. And the reason the answer to this question is basically "none" is their schooling does not teach any of this. They are taught to be surgeons, and through this training it becomes even more difficult for a doctor to view this as a sacred moment—a divine moment for a mother, a child, a family, and humanity.

My impression is that the schooling a typical ob/gyn gets, also deprives them of the information and opportunity to view and treat mother and child wholistically. More often than not, an obstetrician will enter your delivery room, instruct you to lay on your back, instruct you some more (or order you around), treat you as though you are incompetent in a very respectful way, add a dash of fear in case things aren't going as quickly or as planned for them, tell you to push your insides out (when they know nothing about how that feels, if they are male), and then finally pull your baby out of you while they rip you apart, sew you up, and take your baby to poke around his eyes and orifices. You may be lucky enough to be allowed some skin-to-skin greeting and contact with your new baby before they take it away to be washed and measured.

Learn About All Your Options

Knowing that there are other options aside from the hospital experience allows the possibility of inviting a very different birthing experience into your life. Honestly, if I had had the privilege of meeting a mother during my first pregnancy who had had a home birth, and heard about her experiences, I can almost guarantee that I would have delivered at least one of my children at home. Another mother's home birth story would have led me to research and inquire even further, which would have led us to a home birth for sure. But of course I truly have faith in the way my life has played out, and trust why things turned out the way they did. For one, I wouldn't be here writing about the difference between hospital and home births. And so I end this part with a plea to please look into all your options wisely during your first few months of pregnancy. My hope is that every mother can make the best decision for her and her family regarding who will help her deliver her child, and where her baby will be born.

CHAPTER 6

Welcome, Little One

I t was two weeks after my expected due date, and our new medwife simply kept an eye on me twice a week. During our very first meeting with our medwife, we told her to not consider inducing me unless it was absolutely necessary. We also explained that if she did recommend an induction, we wanted to know all our options before we would agree to it. The reason for our decision was that in order to induce, a drug known as Pitocin must be administered.

Pitocin crosses the placenta and can affect a baby for weeks afterwards. Reported effects to a baby are permanent central nervous system damage, neonatal seizures, and even fatalities. (These have been confirmed by the medical community.) I also was worried about my uterus rupturing, which can also occur when Pitocin is administered.

We decided to wait, and three weeks after my due date, the moment arrived when I finally felt unusual cramps around 3:00 a.m. I did get excited, but decided to go back to sleep, because I just knew this was "it." I didn't have any bleeding, and all seemed quite healthy for me and

> **A Little History on Pitocin**
> In 1953, Pitocin was created and was actually approved for the sole use of medical induction and stimulation of labor, not for the use of elective induction as many preg-o's opt for today, thanks to the lack of adequate advice from their doctors. In fact, when it is used for elective induction, i.e., not what it is intended for, that is considered off-label usage of Pitocin. So, based on this information, I'd say no to this drug unless it's absolutely necessary.

the little one—it must have been the beginning of labor! I rested until I couldn't physically sleep anymore, and then at 5:00 a.m. I woke my husband. I told him I was in labor, and of course then he went back to sleep. Oh, was I thankful for Bradley classes, otherwise I would have been smacking my husband and rushing to the hospital, like I had seen in movies.

Mind Over Matter

My point in the following story is to clarify how important mind over matter is, not just during labor, but in everyday life. Once my contractions began, I became extremely excited that we were finally going to meet our child. By 6:00 a.m., I had been having contractions for about an hour, which were about five minutes apart and lasting one minute. This is typically when you should call your midwife or meet her at the hospital. My medwife could hear how happy, calm, and giddy I was over the phone, and she was perplexed. FYI, many believe it's not time to go to the hospital, until you have transformed into a raving monster! Because my contractions were so close, we met at the hospital, and after she examined me, she asked me to do a small meditation. After the meditation, my contractions were irregular, more like 10 minutes apart and just a few seconds long. She kindly suggested that we calm down, go home, and call her when I *had* transformed into a monster.

Labor and Delivery

So we returned home, I took a bath, and then a nice nap. When I woke up we began working through my contractions for as long as I possibly could. We combined walking, drinking, and getting into various positions. Finally I knew I had transitioned when I no longer had control over myself and the contractions. We decided it was time. When we arrived at the hospital, I was 6 centimeters dilated. When you are dilated 6 centimeters or more, it is definitely time to be in the hospital, if you've chosen that route, because things can move pretty quickly from there—at least for many women's labors.

We got into the hospital room's shower, and this was where the medwife examined me from then on until just before the very end of my labor. If I needed to change positions or move around, I would. I discovered that the toilet offered resistance and something to hold onto during the contractions. I would hold the sides and pull myself down thru each one. After several hours, my childhood friend, Olga, arrived. She was everything we needed at the time. She was simply there for whatever came up. She joked around with us, supported us, picked up food for my husband, stroked my hair and face, and took turns massaging my back, because I had back labor and it was intense.

If you cannot hire a doula, I would suggest you bring in that extra person for support—be it your sister, mother, best friend, whomever. A doula is a labor coach, and her main job is to see to a mother's comfort. A doula's support can really move and empower you during labor. Trust me, your husband and you will be very grateful for that extra help, especially if it is your first labor. And since Olga was the godmother-to-be, it was also a special experience for her to be a part of the birth and for us to share it with her.

Every few hours we had to shoo away the anesthesiologist. He kept coming in during my contractions to ask if I would like an epidural. I called him the devil every time and asked him to leave. About 20 hours later, my labor had stalled and I found myself "stuck" at 8 centimeters. After hearing my medwife's reasoning, I finally agreed to try some Pitocin to see if it would help my labor progress. To this day, I say that this is something that should be given to POWs so that they can rapidly release any and all top secret government information. I never imagined pain of this magnitude. Pitocin made the contractions longer and almost constant. I had no break, or breathe, really. And four hours later, I was told that I wouldn't have the energy to push anyway, and to opt for a caesarean. My husband and I were upset, because we were told that our baby's health might be in jeopardy. No one knew why I was stuck, and I ultimately cracked. Just when I had nothing left in me, I screamed to my husband to JUST GET THE BABY OUT! This was right after I kicked my medwife off of me and onto the floor.

And so it was a very quick caesarean. It lasted just a few minutes, and my son didn't make a sound when he was born. My beautiful boy was handed to me in his little blanket—finally he was next to me, face to face, after being "sunny side up" (a.k.a. posterior). I cannot adequately put into words what I was feeling when I saw him for the first time. When I finally held him, it felt like I was holding heaven right in my arms. My husband and I were in love immediately. Our entire life was transformed at that moment.

Shortly after that euphoric, wonderful experience, my husband made sure to follow the nurses everywhere to ensure that no vaccines were given, that there was no bottle feeding, and that my son was brought right back to me. My son stayed with me in my room.

Too often children are taken away from their mothers almost immediately and taken to the nursery for prolonged periods of time, and for reasons that are not life-threatening. Now picture what a shock that is for a newborn soul who only knows the sound, smell and sense of his mother. For nine months, he is in a dark, warm, cozy and safe womb, and now he is exposed to bright lights, an approximately 20-degree drop in temperature, a loud strange place—and he is now being handled in all sorts of ways by complete strangers. Experts agree that it is crucial for your newborn baby to be given to you as quickly as possible and to be comforted, held, fed, and spoken to by you. Attachment parenting must begin immediately if possible. This is the time when primary caregivers, like the mother, respond to their children's immediate and basic needs. This encourages a strong emotional bond to form between the two of you, which provides lifelong consequences. Chances are if you are reading this you have already given birth or are about to. Either way, keep this in mind for your delivery.

Learn, Plan, and Improvise

My birthing experience taught me to never get caught up with one idea or goal, whatever it may be. Life hardly ever goes exactly as planned, since there are lessons to be learned, and growth to be gained. If your plan is to have a natural birth, by all means do what you can to have it that way. But always allow room for flexibility and, more importantly, consider your child's health foremost. If you're in a hospital setting, you will have to do the best you can within that environment. Conventional medicine has its place, as long as we do not misuse or abuse it. I never envisioned myself having to take Pitocin or ending up with a cesarean, but these were my circumstances. I simply did what I had to do in order to have a healthy baby. I know that I did everything in my power at the time to have a natural birth, and that a caesarean is a fine outcome, too.

However, I do feel it is necessary to share important information not available in a system where mothers are left misinformed. It's possible that if I had the necessary information, yes, things could have played out differently—even with a posterior baby. But my family and I obviously had a different path to follow. I personally know several parents who had breeched babies and posterior babies, and whose midwife was qualified enough to turn their baby during labor, which resulted in a natural birth. It is imperative to mention that throughout history and up until recently, obstetricians and midwives were trained to deliver breeched and posterior babies. It was not until just a few decades ago that it was decided that this type of delivery was too much of a risk and would no longer be taught in medical schools. This means that the current new wave of obstetricians are not taught how to deliver babies this way, and are left with no choice but to schedule a cesarean. Midwives, however, are still being trained for this, as they always have, which is why I mention again how crucial it is to invest the time in finding the right person to deliver your child. It will make all the difference.

If you are told that your child is not in the proper position prior to going into labor, you have time to seek assistance in order to turn your baby. Chiropractic adjustments create balance in the pelvis helping babies to assume their optimal positioning. If you have an obstetrician, you can ask him or her to send you to a specialist who will use his or her hands, internally (and sometimes externally), and sonography to encourage your baby to turn. This however may be painful, but well worth the pain if you are scheduled to deliver with a typical ob/gyn and you'd rather deliver naturally. The doctor will likely schedule a cesarean if your baby does not turn within a few days, because your labor has to progress on his terms not your baby's or yours.

A baby will often turn on its own when a mother's pelvis is balanced with chiropractic. Herbs, swimming, walking, and visualization can help turn a baby, too.

In rare cases, the baby will not turn or will even go back to breech position after it has actually been turned. Once again I would say to trust God and your inner guidance. It just may be possible that the baby is uncomfortable and prefers to remain in the breeched position. There have been cases where babies were delivered in breech position because there was an issue with their umbilical cord. In some cases, the cord was too short and was in fact suffocating the baby unless it was in a breech position. And so it would go back to being breeched in order to survive. Being breeched is actually a blessing, in these situations. In many breech situations, something is simply "off," and the baby does not go into the ideal position for delivery. Whether or not it is beneficial for the baby to remain breeched is definitely difficult to assess, but by following your inner voice, research, and a good practitioner, you can make the right decision. Tap into your inner wisdom, your intuition, meditate, pray, and ask for guidance. Remember no one knows better than you.

VBAC and Your Inner Voice

All that being said, I did attempt a VBAC (vaginal birth after caesarean), with my daughter. I felt confident, since studies showed that two-thirds of women attempting a VBAC were successful. Good odds. So with the aid of a very qualified midwifery group, I pushed and pushed for a few hours, but again my daughter was also delivered via c-section. Sometimes I wonder if I am simply not physically able to deliver my babies naturally. Perhaps it has something to do with the shape or size of my pelvis.

I ponder this, because during my labor with my daughter, I pushed for two hours, and she was just stuck. She could not make the dive needed to twirl down the canal. While I was in labor with my daughter, and after she was in the canal for some time, my doula suggested doing a few visualizations. I first visualized and spoke with my daughter, explaining that we will do this together, and there is no need to be afraid. I saw myself holding her little hand and asking her to come out and join us. I then asked her if she wanted to do this, and I felt as if she was too afraid, for whatever reason. When I opened my eyes, I felt a sudden gush of fear inside of me. I told my doula that my daughter didn't want to do this anymore.

I had hardly finished my sentence when a doctor rushed through the door explaining that my daughter's heart rate had dipped, and we needed to go in for an emergency caesarean. Wow, game over. But it was important to be attentive and open to myself, my baby, and the situation. That inner voice and mother-baby connection guided me, and I am grateful that it did.

What Comes With a C-Section

As a mother of two children born via C-section, I will say that there are some side effects for children who enter our world this way. I learned that since their brain and lungs never go through the compression and pressure of natural birthing, their respiratory and digestive systems are not activated like other babies' systems are. The natural birthing process releases certain hormones that stimulate the baby and its organs so they begin to work upon delivery. Studies show that when these hormones are not released, an increase in medical problems, such as asthma, respiratory difficulty for the first few days after delivery. Lung disease, acid reflux, and colic can occur, too.

There's another matter to be aware of. If there are any complications as a result of the caesarean, your child will probably be treated in the Neonatal Intensive Care Unit (NICU) for the first 24 hours. If this happens, the opportunity to bond physically with your child can be delayed and so can breastfeeding. Although this time is crucial for the mother and baby to bond, is obviously not as important as administering emergency medical care. If your baby needs to spend time in the NICU, you may want to incorporate more opportunities over the next six weeks for bonding and helping your child heal from any birth trauma.

Children born by C-section may experience certain sensitivities that a parent should be aware of—and which most babies born naturally do not experience. Even now, I am well aware that my son overreacts hysterically and panics if a shirt gets stuck on his head while he is getting dressed. Other children are very sensitive to touch, since they never experienced that physical forceful compression through the birth canal during delivery. A mindful, gentle, and supportive approach is everything, when it comes to easing your child through these kinds of traumas.

Tools for Healing

I discovered that craniosacral therapy, as well as occupational therapy, can really help heal a traumatic delivery experience. I witnessed my daughter experience the process of a vaginal birth at four months old through the aid of an occupational therapist healer. From that moment on, her colic decreased dramatically, as did her fussiness. I believe that craniosacral therapy helped her release the repressed emotions associated with her birth trauma to the point where she no longer had pent up tensions holding her back socially. She is now known as the "mayor" both in school and our neighborhood.

She also was very fearful as a baby—only to become one of the most fearless children anyone has ever seen. I know this is due to her healing with a shamanic osteopath (see glossary) who helped her in only three short healing sessions.

Chiropractic work has also helped both of my children from the very beginning, right after their arrival and up to this very day. They were adjusted after the squeezing and moving of labor. They are aligned during a cold so that their body and immune system can respond better, and adjusted after little falls here and there. Acupuncture has kept them aligned energetically.

I will also share that, although I did try whatever was in my power and within my knowledge at the time to have a natural birth, I was left with a caesarean experience. Therefore, something needed to restore within me as well. After some time, I did believe that emotionally, I had gotten over what had occurred, only to realize a few years later that there was anger festering deep within me. And this arose in a very subtle way.

Chiropractic and acupuncture are becoming more commonly embraced as health choices for whole families. Modalities such as these are now recognized in the medical field. Although most insurances cover care, chiropractors and acupuncturists offer family wellness type plans so that parents have the option of having care, regardless of their insurance. You can simply contact your insurance carrier for a local practitioner, or ask your community for one they would recommend. Do some research and find one who best suits your family's needs.

Luckily I had the courage to dive in deep within me. I was able to see that I was developing an ambivalent, insecure parenting style as a result of feeling powerless during my first child's delivery. Having the courage and support to heal this was crucial. The more I spoke about the feelings I had, the more support and understanding I received from other moms in my parenting groups. Reading spiritual healing books, like Louise Hay's *You Can Heal Your Life,* also helped me embrace my life's experiences, not judge them, and have faith in the reasons why they came to be. I now see that each experience was there for my growth. It was just a matter of trusting the process. Initially, I found myself stripped of something—something I thought that nature had in store for me and my children, which had instead been taken away from us. Once I made peace with my situation, I realized that these experiences also can bring about profound change not only for us, but for the world around us, too.

Without my going into too much detail, I'm sure you get the idea of how the current system strips away an experience that women were meant to have during their journey here, and their children are affected too. I cannot say that all mothers will feel what I felt, but for those that do, I encourage you to not only allow these feelings to come up and be released, but to also use this experience in a positive way to help raise awareness. Be a part of the shift in consciousness in birthing, in any way you possibly can. Invite yourself to honor your mothering no matter how it is unfolding, and simply dive into this new realm of being with loads of love for yourself and your new family. The rest is truly... history.

Labor Meditation:

During labor, whenever you have a moment to relax, simply close your eyes. Take slow, deep breaths through your diaphragm. Count to 10. As the contractions begin, continue taking long, slow deep breaths. Visualize your hand reaching out to your baby's little hand. Ask your child to come into your arms. Then let your child know that you are there to go through the birthing canal with him or her. You can hold your baby in your arms and picture the two of you diving through the canal head first, and entering this bright world. You are together.

CHAPTER 7

From Career To Motherhood

Since we are on the topic of shifting gears, many of us experience a major transition when we enter into motherhood. I feel the need to address this, just as a "heads up" to a first–timer, or as a consolation to those who are parents already. In today's world, especially in the U.S, before becoming a parent most of us either had a job, career, practice, schooling, or were doing something else that is very different from parenting. Even if you are overjoyed with becoming a mother, you seriously have no idea what hits you, when you become a parent.

Although I am writing about wholistic parenting, I may be giving a confusing impression about who I am. It took me a very long time to get here. My own parents were not "wholistic" per se, but they did come from a culture where parents had no choice but to figure out how to care for, feed, support, and nurse their families with whatever nature provided, as best they could. This created a foundation of what I thought being a parent meant, which did not become clear to me until I became a parent myself.

I grew up and spent most of my years in the United States. Prior to my meeting my husband, I faced many challenges as a young adult, and let's just say that I had to be financially creative in supporting myself, getting my education, and planning my future. Eventually, I became a career woman who simply wanted to start a family, and I faced a few hurdles along that way as well. These struggles brought me to a healthier lifestyle for sure, but for the most part I still enjoyed my career, a very exciting social life with my husband and friends on the weekends, much travel and leisure, and a touch of nature every once in a while. I particularly enjoyed venturing up a mountain trail.

I enjoyed all this thanks to a flexible, lucrative career. In my line of work, as a freelance paralegal, I had developed a great network and had established a strong reputation. I had a very successful situation, where I made my own schedule, worked where I wanted, when I wanted, for whomever I wanted, and charged a wonderful fee for a service that doesn't have much competition. And since I grew to be pretty skillful in my field, I was also able to do work that not very many could do in my small industry. And so I was able to "put my feet up," and truly enjoy what I had created.

The pace of my life was fast, but I liked it that way. For balance, I also took many vacations every year. I was always a multi-tasker and an achiever. When I would share about my day with a friend, I would realize only by their reaction how much I actually managed to do in one day. In fact, my friends seemed to always wonder how it was possible to pack so much in. You get the picture.

When my son was born, I planned to return to work by the time he was three months old. I had no idea what lay ahead of me. I wish someone had told me that my life would come to a screeching halt, and my entire life would just be baby and nothing but baby. First of all, I basically lived in my pajamas and did not leave my house for the first three months. Some of you may relate to this, and some may not. My plan to return to my "normal" lifestyle was no longer a reality.

This wasn't even a gear shift—I just stopped short! Forget multi-tasking, forget my independence, and forget my sense of self. So much had changed. I had to learn how to depend on someone else to make my food, clean my clothes, pay my way, and so much more. I even remember a time when my mother fed me my breakfast during the first week. I was unrecognizable—to myself and to anyone else around me. Simple things like a shower had become a luxury. I would have loved it if even one of the books I read had prepared me for this chaos. None of them even suggested how dramatically life could change. It was startling and completely unexpected. Through talking to friends in my community, I realized that what I was going through was normal. Although I did find some comfort in that, it still did not feel normal to me.

I was lucky that my son was cute and oozed love, because he made it all seem okay. After the first month, my mother had to return to Europe, and I felt adrift when she left. I had to figure out how to go about my daily life in a whole new way. This seemed like an overwhelming task, given that I had figured out everything once and had been happy with my life. In my sleep-deprived, half-zombie state I wore the same clothes for days, barely had time for a shower, and rarely socialized on the phone or in person. I also didn't cook, clean, run errands, or do anything else that had been a part of my typical day.

As for my financial luxury, well that changed just as quickly. My husband left his partnership and ventured off on his own just a few days after my son was born. There were no jobs lined up for him, and, as a freelance paralegal, my income stopped as soon as my maternity leave started. We suddenly had to figure out how to make ends meet, while trying to also live a wholistic lifestyle. Eventually I learned that breastfeeding is such a gift financially, because I did not have to buy formula, bottles, accessories, and natural remedies. All I needed was diapers and wipes. With my daughter I used cloth diapers, and so we saved even more money with our second child.

Since my son only wanted to be with me, I didn't need all the contraptions that keep a baby "entertained." I did not have a play pen, swing, or anything other than my carriers, some blankets for the floor, and a little play gym from my baby shower. I also eventually learned that I could pay less on medical insurance, since I hardly ever needed the aid of a pediatrician, nor did I use prescription drugs. Whatever money we saved went to supplements, essential oils, and good food.

I understood that as long as my children were in a healthy environment, ate a healthy diet, and had clean natural medical remedies, their bodies would grow stronger, and would fight and process illnesses better. A friend once asked how I could afford a $50 bottle of essential oil as a stay-at-home mom. I replied, "I could have gone to the doctor and spent $30 on my co-pay, and then another $30 on a prescription that would have lasted me anywhere from a week to a month. My oil will last me several months, saves me a doctor's visit, and I don't have to worry about possible pharmaceutical side effects."

I've always weighed things out that way. If I'm simply dealing with a runny nose and a cough, I know it's something I can handle. If my child's health is regressing and I am not able to treat it, then I would seek immediate help. I am proud to share that my children enjoy great health, and I believe it is as a result of our lifestyle. As we explored simpler, healthier, and more enjoyable ways to live as a family, we turned to natural remedies, organic food, a balanced diet low in sugars, coupon shopping, and rarely eating in restaurants.

Time passed by and, although I had initially intended to return to work after three months, I realized that I was not ready to leave my son when that time came. Although I didn't want to leave my child, I could not see how I could possibly stay home when my husband's career was going through so much transition—he was just starting his company. Because I wasn't bringing in any income, I felt guilty whenever I thought about being a stay-at-home mom.

However, the thought did keep coming up, and so it deserved a conversation. It wasn't easy, but after many talks and even arguments, my husband and I decided that it was best for our son and me if I stayed home. Although I was already saving money from breastfeeding, natural healing, using coupons, and working as my husband's new secretary from home, I looked into more ways to save. I began to compare prices more, shop during sales, and basically do anything that helped us cut down on expenses. It didn't feel so good at first, but I knew that at least I was home with my baby, and I was following my gut about it. I had no regrets, and I enjoyed our time together.

This was my way, and I know of other moms who found their own way. Many worked from home, making calls while nursing, for instance. Others moved in with family, some built websites and started blogs, and the list goes on. But it all came from intuition, empowered by intention and honesty. As my father always said, "If there's a will, there's a way." I have found that to be true.

Let Go of Guilt

Although this worked for me, you may feel called to go back to work within the first few months after childbirth. If so, please be fair to yourself and take some time to honestly examine how you feel about this decision. Once you have looked at all your options, explored your feelings, and are free from guilt, you will know at the deepest level whether this is the best decision for you and your family. Do what seems best intuitively. This is what intuitive parenting is all about. And if feelings of guilt arise, remind yourself that having a job outside of the home does not make you a second-rate mother, and that your children will not have a second-rate experience. Do not blame yourself for having a career.

Unfortunately, I often sense guilt in moms who have returned to work. I suggest that they either let go of the guilt, or reevaluate their options. It's never too late to have a conversation with your husband, boss, family members, or anyone else who can assist, if you want to consider the possibility of being home with your children more. One of my very close friends evaluated her family's needs with her husband, and they jointly decided that she would return to work for a few days a week. Dad changed his schedule to stay home one weekday, and grandpa spends two days with the baby. This worked like a charm for their family, and is a great example of a way to bring everyone in to help so that mom can have more time at home with the baby.

After my daughter turned three, I returned to work part-time. Personally, it feels great knowing that I had those years with my kids, and now they are off to school. I am excited to be back to work again. It was an interesting ride in itself, and a good one overall, filled with many great memories to last us all a lifetime.

It is hard to imagine what it will be like when you become a parent. It is also hard to believe that everything can change overnight. I will never forget the initial shock and experience. Looking back, I see that our lives changed irrevocably the moment our son arrived. But don't let this scare you. I can reassure you that there is a way through this major adjustment that will be right for you. I can also reassure you that this transition can awaken a whole new side of you, and show you a beautiful, new side of your innate potential. I have realized that our baby is not the only one who was thrust into a brand new world; we were too. It's a new and dynamic way of life for the entire family. Everyone gets reacquainted with themselves and their loved ones. The family is birthed into a new life. And in the same way that every baby-birthing story is different, so too is every family birthing story.

Any way it happens, it is beautiful, and I say congratulations to all! Have fun and see what grows out of this awesome responsibility and adventure.

CHAPTER 8

The Next 30 Days

The time after birth is a time for mother and child to bond. It's also a time of healing, adjustment, hormonal balancing, family integration, and a whole new experience for the new parents. Because this new family dynamic will continue to change—and is in itself in its infancy—the transition to parenthood, including the needs of the mother and baby during the post-partum period, should be treated with thoughtfulness. For thousands of years the people in most countries have considered the post-partum time to be a sacred time. When proper attention is given at this period of time, it decreases the chance that a new mother will face more complications, such as postpartum depression, breastfeeding issues, hormonal imbalances, fussy babies, and even abandoned newborns.

What It Is All About

This sacred time has been valued throughout the world's cultures, and throughout various religions, as a very important time for a new family. I believe this still is true. Anthropological case studies reveal how many cultures have different names for the first 30- to 40-day period after birth. In Latin America, they call it *La Cuarentena,* which is a 40-day quarantine period, when mother and infant rest from their long, challenging journey, and have a chance to get acquainted. It's a time for others to help care for the new mother and baby with home meals, home remedies, and taking care of household duties.

In the Bible, there is a passage in Leviticus that says that 40 days of purification are needed after the birth of a son, and double that after a daughter. In China, starting from the Sung Dynasty, there is a term for postpartum called "doing the month," which involves basically the same idea: keeping it all to a minimum while receiving help from others. In Greece, it's called "the forty days." Other countries refer to this time as "lying-in," and places such as India, Africa, and the Middle East have their own practices for this time. A mother needs this time physically, since her body has just undergone one of the most intense experiences, whether it was a vaginal birth, a home birth, water birth, Cesarean, or whatever. A mother also needs the time emotionally and spiritually, so that she is able to tune into her own needs as well as her infant's. This helps ensure their success on this new journey.

Two great articles that explain in a helpful way the importance of staying home to recover for the next six weeks are "Revisioning Postpartum Care in the United States: Global Perspectives," by Jade Groff[3] and "Mothering the Mother: The Importance of Postpartum Care, by Rev. Pilar (Ma'at) Grant.[4]

This six-week time period is just another wonderful tradition that we have honored from the beginning of our time as humans. Once again, we have turned away from what we have always done, which has led us to depression and disconnection from our children. I will not get into all the details of such an important practice here, and leave it to the articles mentioned above to elaborate. If you would like more support on this topic, I encourage you to do your own research.

How This Tradition Fits in Today's World

Although I hardly left the house, and was very challenged after my son was born, I did wish I was able to simply be out and about and go to the market and do all the normal things I was used to doing. My mother kept insisting that I respect this time and leave all that aside so that I could honor this time with my child. I did end up staying home with

---

3   www.Instituteof Midwifery.org

4   www.mothering.com/community/a/mothering-the-mother

my child, but mostly because it just flowed that way for me due to all the difficulty. I can't really say that I initially connected with the idea of this tradition at all. Later on it was a choice only because I wanted this time with my son—it wasn't because of the tradition. I find that most mothers I meet, feel disconnected form this tradition, too, and find it hard time to stay home with their child for an entire month. I figured it was just modern day life, until I met mothers from other countries who told me otherwise.

What I slowly learned is that the rest of the world does honor this post-partum period in various ways. For example, in Sweden, all working parents are entitled to sixteen months paid child leave. Wow, both parents get to stay home and support their new infant and new family. And in other countries such as Slovakia, a mother has three years paid leave. In fact, as a nation, the U.S. stands out for its lack of government-sponsored support for mothers and babies during the postpartum period. In comparison to the rest of the world, we rank badly when it comes to parental leave and parental support. There are only four countries in the entire world that have no laws mandating paid time off for new parents, Liberia, Swaziland, Papua New Guinea, and our own nation. So in most of the world, the new family is valued and the pressure to resume life as it was before, is minimal. Everyone has a chance to adapt, enjoy, and even invest time in their new family. Most of the world agrees that this time is crucial for all new families and all new citizens and new souls entering our world, with the exception of a few other countries and the United States. From time to time, I ponder the effect this has on the next generation and ourselves as new parents.

Ways to Create Your Own Version of Baby Mooning

Since this time of "lying-in" is not really practiced in the U.S., if a family intends to follow a period of baby mooning (as we call it), they will have to create one for themselves. In addition to whatever you decide, you may need to set expectations with well-meaning family members so that they are aware of the boundaries you think will be most helpful to you after your baby arrives. It's likely that you will need to set yourself up as much as possible beforehand. Otherwise, you may have no choice but to have your extended family sleeping in your living room during this period.

Here are a few ideas in addition to what your midwife or health care professional has already suggested to you. And what is more important, use whatever suggestions come to mind from within you first and foremost. Here are a few suggestions.

Stock Up on Healthy Food

When you are close to your due date, take some time to prepare a few nutritious meals, which you can freeze and have available for at least the first week after childbirth. Soups, like chicken soup, are best. Because they contain a lot of liquid and nutrients, they also help with your milk production and nursing success. You can also store loads of soup in your freezer. Big meals like casseroles will help add some variety, and give you lots to choose from later. Purchase a bunch of boxes of crackers and a bag of apples. These will come in handy on your night table and allow you to simply reach over and snack, even if your baby has fallen asleep in your arms. Make sure that you speak with your health care professional about taking a nutritional supplement formula during your postpartum period. Often this will help rebalance your hormones, so that your cycles and hormone levels return to what they were prior to your pregnancy. Keep a good supply of supplements, put them in a pill box, and have them ready to take for each day.

During Pregnancy, our hormones reach and fluctuate at very different levels in order to support the pregnancy. These hormonal imbalances are quite common and often cause a variety symptoms, including mood swings, depression, thyroid issues, and more. In some cases, a woman's hormones will never go back to exactly what they were before. With the aid of a good supplement protocol, you can bring those hormones back to normal levels really quickly. This can be crucial if a mom is experiencing symptoms of post-partum depression and other issues.

Accept Help

Ask for help from your husband or partner, and one more person.

Because I had been so independent, I found this suggestion hard to listen to, however, it really makes all the difference. Choose someone you trust and love, who is not judgmental, and who can offer up some of their time. For example, if a friend can come by once a day and tackle one small chore, like putting in a load of laundry or cleaning the dishes, it will be a blessing and a lot more support than your realize.

There will be plenty of things that your husband or partner can help with. I believe that most of our husbands and partners want to support us and be included during this transition. There is a good chance that he will want to feel needed, so help him figure out how he can contribute now that the family's needs are different. I was surprised by how much my husband stepped up to the plate, when I went from stubbornly independent to needy. When it comes to their baby, most dads are all in—they just might need some guidance and support to be able to take on chores and tasks they have never done before.

Be accepting of whatever help you get and be patient. It won't always be exactly what you want or how you would do it. That's okay. Just speak up about what you need.

The next piece of advice is to sleep when the baby sleeps. Although I heard this from a number of experienced people, I admit that I didn't take the suggestion seriously until I almost passed out from exhaustion. Whatever it is, trust me when I say most of what you think you have to do is not that necessary or serious, and can wait. I eventually got to the point where everything had to wait, because I couldn't function from the sleep deprivation.

Relax and Enjoy the Ride

And so although I didn't exactly have a cultural connection to the tradition of staying home for the first month, I chose to create what felt right for me and my family. My gears did shift from fifth gear to first. I had no choice but to surrender to it. And so if you find that you need or choose to do the same, there are ways to plan ahead for this change and live in simplicity for the first month or few months. I didn't even go to the grocery store. I ordered everything from Fresh Direct.com. It was organic, fresh, healthy, and delivered right at my door. In fact, everything was delivered to my door. Anything I needed for myself or our baby was ordered via phone or Internet, and came to my door. I stayed home, and focused on myself, our baby, and our family. In the long run, you will be so happy that you put your time and attention towards nurturing yourself and getting acquainted with your baby's cues, personality, and needs. With each sacrifice I made, I found I was falling deeper and deeper in love. I think you will too.

Meditation

If you find yourself feeling overwhelmed by life and all that needs to be done, sit down, relax, and take in a few long deep breaths, followed by long exhales. Ask the universe for help to see you through this time. Trust that it will all be okay and will work out somehow. Know that you and your baby are safe, loved, and cared for, and all your obstacles will soon disappear.

Repeat: All is well in my world. All is well in my world.

You can also say this with conviction during a three-minute meditation. Simply place your palms together over your heart, with your thumbs touching your chest. Repeat this for three minutes and then open your eyes.

PART 2

Now What Do We Do?

CHAPTER 9

Spiritual Parenting Inside the Womb and Out

"The only real valuable thing is intuition."
Albert Einstein

Because of my two children and pregnancies, I have been able to reopen my heart to the universe. Both children play a very different role, and are slightly different teachers to me. Both have led me closer to my Self, to my Source, and to our world. During both my pregnancies, I enjoyed communicating with my unborn children through visualizations, meditations, and Reiki treatments. I first saw my son during a Reiki session, and my daughter, during a sacred moment—and those were the most beautiful memories of my pregnancies. I will forever remember when I first saw my son's profile, during my first Reiki session. I felt pure bliss, and it made me very emotional.

Through the help of my doula, I frequently met with my daughter during visualizations. I would comfort her and hold her hand as we envisioned her birthing together. I often visually entered a safe garden where I would ask all my loved ones to guide both my daughter and me through a healthy pregnancy and delivery. I believe my daughter sent this doula. This woman had very strong spiritual beliefs—so much so that she healed her own breast cancer.

Her confidence in her beliefs allowed me the opportunity to begin stretching my own beliefs to where they used to be, and even further.

This allowed me to connect with my daughter, and eventually reconnect with my own spirituality so that I could understand my daughter. She is a very powerful little soul who does not allow me to doubt my spirituality. Her presence and her ways remind me of what is true and to never doubt it. She responds to my thoughts and emotions throughout each day. Both my children and I are also very connected in our dream states, and the next day we reveal to each other similar memories from the night before. I am deeply thankful to them for helping me strengthen my connection to our Divine Source.

Deep Sense of Knowing

As I mentioned, I had sensed my son's gender before his birth. In a different fashion, I also knew we were having a girl when I was pregnant with my daughter. It took longer for me to get this sense during my second pregnancy. I was five months pregnant and still had no awareness of whether we were having a boy or a girl. During a vacation, I was sitting out under the afternoon Greek sun while my son was napping. I was reading a spiritual book, and I was suddenly distracted by an unexpected wind that came by and blew the weeds in front of me. I closed my eyes and enjoyed this beautiful feeling of comfort, relief, and security. Suddenly within me, I saw a little girl giggling with her hands touching her face—as if being silly with me and mocking me for not "knowing" yet. When I opened my eyes, I was so happy, I ran in the house, called my husband, and told him: "We are having a girl!"

I strongly encourage every pregnant mother to meditate and visualize throughout their nine months of pregnancy. This will not only help you bond with your child during the most important time of both of your lives, but it will also enable you to reconnect with yourself. It will create the space to begin nurturing and communicating with your child from the very beginning, and will also raise the volume on your intuitive voice, which you will need for what lies ahead of you.

This is not something that should be rare or unusual, although it seems that way to most of us. I believe that our current society has robbed many women of their mothering instinct. If we allow ourselves to listen to our intuition once again, we may just surprise ourselves. Every single mother is able to sense when her child is in need of her or in some sort of distress, even if her child is nowhere near her. We all can be very much connected to our children, as well as to each other, as we are all one. And now more than ever, the universe has allowed us the space to make this possible again.

Shift in Consciousness

Right now, there is a shift in consciousness happening for all of us. This is something that we are presently creating and co-creating. As humanity evolves, so do our parenting practices. We are highly intellectual, spiritual beings, with the ability to fuse together all that we have learned to date and apply it, not to shut down one or the other parts of ourselves. It is time that we embrace this. In brief, if we integrate our mind, body and spirit, as well as utilize all that we have learned and created throughout evolutionary history, we can achieve great possibilities as people, and ultimately as role models to future generations. When we tap into our whole being, we can create a better future and a better world, giving our children the tools and potential to fulfill their own higher good as well.

How do we do this? I started by reading moving and enlightening books, finding those with which I really resonated. After experiencing the light than shone on me when I was reading these books and absorbing the wisdom on their pages, I gained a deeper understanding of my soul and purpose. I found it difficult to hold onto this state of being in the midst of all of life's hurdles. A wise teacher once advised me on how I could preserve my connection to my deeper consciousness, despite what the outside world was throwing at me. She suggested I meditate. When I did, I would feel my connection to our Source, and ultimately I would make this knowledge my *own*. This would no longer be knowledge passed onto me, but would become *part of me*. And if I couldn't meditate at first, I should attempt chanting, as this is a way of helping the mind to be still and relaxed.

If you enjoy music, and have a hard time meditating, then try chanting. It is easy, fun, and it takes you to a meditative state rather quickly and effortlessly. It's a great way to begin training the mind to be still—but you will notice it goes even further than that, and works sort of like an affirmation, rewiring your brain and whole being. My personal favorites are the chants by Snatam Kaur and Krishna Das. They are highly vibrational, and easy to chant along with, not to mention beautiful. My kids love chanting along with me because they love any kind of music. My daughter asks for her kundalini chants by Snatam Kaur every morning in the car.

Meditations and prayer have helped me many times, too. When my first child is struggling with a phase, testing me, and generally being difficult, I usually pray before I retire to bed. I ask his guardian angel to guide him (and me) through this difficult time, help him be at peace, and support him while he lives his journey as he chooses. Most of the time, when he wakes up the next morning, there is a dramatic difference in his behavior, and it lasts for quite some time. I have also prayed to God and my angels for guidance during difficult times in my marriage and when parenting. I have always been answered, guided, and helped with my struggles when I do this.

Integrating Your Spirituality and Parenting

It is important to remember that we are all human, and we all bump heads with one another from time to time. If we keep allowing this to happen with no remedy, eventually there will be a wound. And if that wound is constantly poked, then it has no opportunity to heal and may only grow larger and deeper. Just remember to tap in to your intuition. You may even want to do some internal cleaning if needed, since this will make room for more good to come into your life. The idea is to get away from "stacking and packing in" more than you can handle, because it will weigh you down. Lighten up and model this to your children, so that they gain the tools and practices they need to find inner peace and coexist with others without strife.

There are so many ways to clear your space. The one that is "best" depends on what resonates and works for you. Here are some modalities I have used to clear my blocks and negativity: You can write and let it all out, practice forgiveness in your visualizations by forgiving those who have harmed you and releasing them, do chakra cleansing, Reiki, affirmations, visualizations, intuitive healing, holistic psychology, group workshops, girl's night out, couple workshops and retreats, using homeopathic remedies, shamanic healing, and craniosacral therapy. I have tried these different modalities as a way to release anything that is holding me back in my life or in my relationships. I want to continue to grow and move towards my full potential, so I can live life more fully. I want this for my children and for you as well.

Whenever my husband or I have benefited from these healing modalities, we have seen these benefits trickle down to our children, too. Our shift almost immediately causes a shift in our children's behavior. That is because our children absorb our experiences on a conscious and subconscious level, and reflect them back to us. It is amazing to notice this. Once my husband and I began embracing and processing our anger, we noticed that our children were showing no signs of aggression. In fact, whatever emotion my husband and I are experiencing individually and between us, our children display it immediately between each other and their peers. For example, the love that my husband and I feel for each other has deepened so much as of late. Recently, my son's teacher told us that our son has grown into a very compassionate and affectionate child, and is like this with everyone around him.

Now that my son is older, I enjoy a nighttime prayer with him, often after we read a book together. What his pure, loving mind prays for literally blows my mind, touches my heart, and humbles me. Sometimes he even cracks me up. He asks for rain for our vegetable garden, for God to watch over all earth's animals, "even the ones that bite." He is thankful for his family (especially his "silly little sister"), and everyone in the world he doesn't know, for builders and homes, and so much more. We chant together, occasionally do yoga together, and mostly snuggle a lot. I've always envisioned walking the spiritual path as a family, and now I am enjoying the reality of it.

Meditation:

Close your eyes, relax and take a few intentional breaths. Ask your Self for the support to speak your truth, be your truth, and live your truth. Try this for several weeks and see what unfolds.

Meditation in Times of Struggle:

If you are having struggles with someone, relax, close your eyes, and see yourself facing this other person. Say, "Let there be light," and envision a bright yellow light shining between the two of you. Do this for a few nights. Next, close your eyes again, and see yourself with that same person and say, "Let there be water." Do this for a few nights. Finally, close your eyes again and see the two of you again. Say, "Let there be land," and do this for a few nights. This practice allows the possibility for light to shine on your problem, water to clear it all out, and land to surface underneath you so that there are new possibilities between the two of you.

CHAPTER 10

Sleeping

If you are a parent, or about to become one, you have probably heard a lot of advice about sleeping, and some of it is contradictory. Obviously, sleep is an integral part of health, and what you do with your newborn can have long-term effects. As a new mom, I worried about which approach to take because of what the consequences could be. This left my husband and I feeling very confused, to say the least. If we co-sleep (have our baby in the bed with us), will the baby ever sleep on his own in his own room? On the other extreme, if the baby cries it out in the middle of the night and we do not go to him, will we risk developing a detached relationship with our child? Worse yet, will he feel lonely or abandoned, unsafe and unsecure? This is not the message I wanted to instill during those first few precious and critical months.

Honestly, I have done it all, and it all works in its own way. Initially, I had my son in a co-sleeper bed, only because he wanted to nurse all night and all day due to his acid reflux, and I was exhausted. He would wake every hour and sometimes more often than that. So by the third month, I began having him just sleep right next to me in my bed instead of in the co-sleeper bed. The way that sleeping situation began is when he would fall asleep in my arms, and I would barricade myself with body pillows and with the co-sleeper bed next to me so that he wouldn't slip away. Because of the reflux, I would sleep sitting up with him in my arms, to minimize the reflux. We would both wake up and find that neither of us had moved an inch. This is great for a baby with reflux, but does not feel good to a mom's neck and shoulders, if she's always in a stiff position.

Eventually, I tried sliding down in my bed more, little by little, until he finally began sleeping next to me. I had his upper chest elevated for his reflux with a special reflux pad from the baby store, and when he would wake, he would nurse and go back to sleep. I hardly woke up—just enough to get him comfortably latched on, since I have a small chest, and he had to work hard to find me. The elevation helped with my small breasts as well, since he could reach my elevated nipple. So our co-sleeping began and lasted up until he was seven months old.

The Methods That Work Best for You

At that time, I had read a few great books about sleeping, such as the *No Cry Sleep Solution* by Elizabeth Pantley and *The Baby Sleep Book* by Dr. William Sears. I took notes and tweaked their suggestions, according to what best suited my family and my relationship with my son. During our co-sleeping, I used Pantley's notes to help my son accept a pacifier in place of my nipple. I also tried to teach him to not wake up to nurse after he fell asleep. For this, Pantley advised that once the baby is well fed, comforted and is asleep, to slip out your nipple and put slight pressure on his chin in order to keep his mouth closed when he tries to open up and look for your nipple again. If you repeat this something like 50 times, eventually the baby will catch on and not look to nurse again after you pull your nipple away. I was also trying to break the strong nurse-to-sleep habit and association that he had developed.

Once he was seven months though, he began to wake every 15 minutes to nurse. This lasted for a few weeks and it was torture for me. My husband decided to move to the couch, which was extremely uncomfortable, and I developed pretty bad sleep anxiety. I was actually waking up every 15 minutes, even if my son had not woken up yet—and sometimes I woke him up instead because of my own movements. With all that extra nursing, when he was not hungry and just using the breast for comfort, my son began spitting up the excessive amount of milk he was taking in all night, and this was worsening his reflux. Co-sleeping was clearly no longer working, and it was time for a change.

What Changed

So our ritual went something like this: Our evening routine remained the same as it was from the very beginning when he was just a few weeks old. From my son's very first month of life, we developed a sweet nighttime routine right after dinner. We would read a book, then go off to a warm bath, followed by a nice massage. After the bath, he would then have mommy's milk and snuggles and then bedtime.

At seven months, things changed, and instead of that routine, I would go to his room for bedtime. I would begin by sitting in a chair by his crib, so that transport from the chair to his bed did not involve too many steps and movement. While nursing I also had a noise machine going, which I used for naps and nighttime. I always preferred the sounds of water or rain.

I purchased dark blue curtains to darken his room and set the mood. I also bought many pacifiers of the kind he finally took to. There are so many options for BPA-free pacifiers now, so you can pacify without introducing any toxicity. We spent a lot of time in his room. While nursing, I would hum a nursery song and pat his bottom. When he would drift off to sleep, I would place him in his crib by first laying down his bottom and then slowly letting go of

For the baby's first body wash, I suggest castile soap, because it has nothing toxic in it, and is gentle on a baby's sensitive skin. I also used organic jojoba oil for massage and moisturizing, which has nothing in it other than the oil itself. To make sure your baby gets the most out of his bath time, I would also recommend a shower filter. The water supplied to the majority of homes in the U.S., and pours out of your faucets, has chlorine, fluoride, and other toxins. Not only do they dry out a baby's skin, these toxins are also much more harmful when absorbed by a young, pure body than when absorbed by a grown, healthy adult.

A Word About Fluoride

If you visit the site, www.fluoridealert.org, you should find a few excerpts from a fluoride alert that briefly explains how important it is to filter your home's water. The site references numerous world studies that show how fluoride-treated water (at levels as low as 1 ppm) can impact and lower children's IQ, enter and damage the fetal brain and brain tissue, and impair learning his head. I would never actually take my palm off his butt though. When he was finally in his bed and did not wake during the transfer, I would very softly and gently pat his butt, and continue humming until I knew he was asleep. Then I would lift my hand slowly, one finger at a time. When my whole hand was finally off his bottom, I would very slowly lift it away, and eventually I did the same with my whole body. Since they can sense our warmth, smell us, and have us on their "baby radar," I would keep on humming until I was out of his room. This worked pretty well at night, and he would sleep for two hours straight at first. When he woke up, I would bring him into my bed for the remainder of the night.

and memory, in addition to many other harmful effects. It also states that "parents or caregivers may not notice the symptoms associated with mild fluoride toxicity or may attribute them to colic or gastroenteritis, particularly if they did not see the child ingest fluoride."[5] I believe if you visit the site for more information, you will be surprised by what you learn.

Noise Machines help muffle out any noisy floor creaks as you're leaving the baby's room or any other normal house noise. You can find these at Wal-Mart, a baby store, Brookstone, and even at a big-box home store, like Bed, Bath & Beyond.

Nap Time May Be A Bit Different

The next step was to smooth out the nap times. Here I had to allow for some crying. He expressed himself very well because he did not like this new routine and knew this was not our usual scenario. I would nurse and conduct the whole ritual, but he would wake up the minute he touched the mattress. If he did, I gave him his pacifier, and literally went into the crib with him while he cried and fussed (this I got from *The Baby Whisperer Book*). I would hug, kiss, snuggle, sing, and softly say that "Mommy is here, I love you, and this is for your best." I did whatever I could to help him understand that the other way no longer worked, and that I was here to

---

5   Shulman, J.D., Wells, L.M. "Acute fluoride toxicity from ingesting home-use dental products in children, birth to 6 years of age." *Journal of Public Health Dentistry* 57 (1997): 150-8.

help him through this transition. I would not leave his side as he worked through this.

I ran everything by my husband so I knew we would approach the sleep problem consistently, and so that I could have a break during the anticipated first few rough nights. He read the books, was in agreement, and took turns with me when our son woke up at night. By the third night, my son pulled his very first six hours of sleep in his crib—in his room. For real! Does this all actually work? Wow! I was ecstatic, and my husband and I looked forward to having a life again. By the third night and by the time he was a year old, he was sleeping beautifully. Twelve hours of sleep at night, with a two-hour nap during the day. My son rocks!

All Children are Different

Each child is different. With my daughter, it only took one night. She never took a pacifier. She instead preferred that we rub her lower back and bottom to sleep. She didn't depend on this to sleep when she would wake up at night; rather it was what helped her drift off in the beginning of the night. At two years old, she still woke up once a night every so often but now at four years old, she is champion sleeper. Like my son, she too had begun waking every 20 minutes when she was 7 months old. I used essential oils to help her ease off to sleep quickly and comfortably. I would apply a drop of Young Living's lavender oil on the bottom of her feet and behind her ears. I would also diffuse the oils all night. This helped tremendously, and luckily, she did catch on very quickly.

By the time children are three years old, they begin to settle and sleep through the night. So if you'd like your child to sleep all night prior to that, it's a high expectation, and you may be setting yourself up for disappointment.

What Works For Me, May or May Not Work for You

No one is sure why some children sleep all night from their first day, and why some still wake up by the age of four. However, research does show that the majority of babies should begin sleeping through the night from the age of nine months. That never really meant much to me, though. Again, each child is different and so is each family. Many variables are also at play. The basic standard is to simply follow a good nighttime routine, and don't add too many dependencies, such as mommy, pacifier, and nursing. The idea is that if your child grows dependent on anything to fall asleep, then he will always need mommy, her milk, her scent, the pacifier, or nursing, a certain type of music, dad, or even the antics of an older sibling in order to fall asleep—hence the term "sleep dependency." My suggestion is that you do whatever works so that both parent and child sleep. When you are up for some changes and modifications, then go for it and hope for the best! Keep in mind that it may take a while, weeks or months, to teach your child something new and to break old habits.

A Splash of Spirituality at Play

As a parent who always seeks wholistic approaches and intuitive guidance to approach our parenting challenges, I am inclined to share that there was a spiritual remedy for my daughter's sleepless nights. Once she was about 15 months, I had reached my limit of sleeping on the floor in her room, while my hand would grow numb through her bed rails as I held her hand to sleep or rubbed her back. My husband and I missed each other, I had seen my chiropractor way too many times during the last year, and honestly, I had to pull myself together in order to function for my family. I could not drive my son to school on three to four hours of sleep much longer. I had reached the end of my rope, and so I began asking in my prayers and meditations for guidance through this challenge. Specifically, I wanted to understand what would be the best way to ease my daughter into independent sleep.

The answer came quickly. Within a few days I began experiencing random, excruciating uterine pain. Eventually my entire body was immobile from the pain, but the uterine part was indescribable. I told my husband that this might be the first time he would ever have to drive me to the emergency room. I can usually handle pain, but this was unbearable. While having this random, mysterious, and painful experience, I still had to sleep on the floor in my daughter's room, only that I was curled up in a fetal position from the pain. When she would wake up, I couldn't move over to put my hand through the rail, and so I just began telling her "It's sleep time," and that "Mommy loves you."

Being that she is very intuitive, she sensed something was off with me, and to my surprise and relief she went back to sleep in less than a minute. No fuss. This went on for three nights. Since everything had gone so smoothly and she was sleeping, the fourth night I just decided to sleep in my bed, and voila, she did not wake up at all that night. And by then the uterine pain had coincidentally disappeared as well.

I suddenly understood why that painful experience took place. I feel that I was literally brought to a physically immobile situation by the universe in order to be able to help my daughter ease into sleep (as well as myself). I don't believe it was a coincidence that of all random things I had intense uterine or womb pain and was not able to move. Since the uterus symbolizes birth, motherhood, and children, this part of me had to get my attention and keep sharing its message with me until I finally heard it.

I had no choice but to comfort my daughter by staying close to her, letting her know I was there and I loved her. I could no longer touch her to provide extra security while she was sleeping, because the pain was so intense that it kept me from being able to physically give her my hand. On some level, I think she knew that it was time, and that I could no longer enable her sleep dependency. She responded immediately, and in no time she was able to sleep on her own. And that was it. She's been sleeping on her own ever since. I appreciated the helping hand from above, and I thanked God and my Self for the help.

This Too Shall Pass

Our invented method of sleep training was difficult, but it did work for our family. The wholistic approach was just as challenging, but at least it was not as emotional or traumatic for the kids (and ourselves). They were never left alone to figure it out. We were right there the whole time during their learning process. And in the end the methods for both children proved successful. They are healthy and deep sleepers. The important part is to find out exactly what works best so that there is no brewing resentment between any family members or towards yourself. And if you can't figure out what to do, then don't forget to ask for a little help from friends, family, loved ones, community, your Self, and God. You'll be amazed at the response.

As for my sleep anxiety, it was so bad that after my son was soundly asleep all night, I would shoot up from bed anyway every 15 minutes. It was horrible. I found that essential oils and Bach flower remedies healed my problem. With my son, I would take a few drops of White Chestnut and Oak Bach flower remedies before I went to bed and whenever I would wake. With my daughter, I also used lavender oil on the bottom of my feet and the essential oil Peace and Calming under my nose and behind my ears. I also diffused these oils all night in my room as well as in my daughter's room, to ensure a nice, healing, and deep sleep. Within a few weeks I was sleeping all night and haven't had a problem since. Life was finally back to normal.

CHAPTER 11

Holding And Warmth

More Than Just Warmth

Warmth isn't merely a physical sensation. We all need a combination of love, which is emotional warmth, and touch, which is physical warmth. Ultimately, when we hold our warm, cozy infant we enjoy the exchange of love that flows between parent and child. Many consider this healing warmth, and I believe it is. I also know that it provides security and comfort. Keeping our children warm and holding them near us is a crucial part of their survival and development. Skin to skin contact with a parent is what has saved many dying children in hospitals and adoption homes. It is something that moms can easily offer to their child at any time. In addition to this loving warmth, physical warmth makes all the difference in their physical development – especially in the first few years of their life. This begins from the moment our children are born.

During his first day of life, I was told that my son had to be taken away for one hour during the visiting hours as it was hospital policy. Within minutes, we heard a baby crying so loudly that my husband went to check to see if our baby was making all that noise—and he was! I simply had to go into the nursery and stay with him, nurse him, and hold him, as my husband entertained our family members with our birthing story in my room. Of course, if mom is not able to be with her baby for a good reason, there is no need to feel guilty. Mom needs to heal properly in order to enjoy the many beautiful moments to come.

One thing every parent learns is that babies and children are very resilient. This comes as a big surprise, because we know they are also quite vulnerable. However, if we can, we should do our best to respond to our baby's cues, right from the beginning.

Physical Warmth

After you have delivered, you will probably notice that your newborn was brought to you dressed very warmly with a cap on his or her head. If you delivered during a heat wave you may wonder why your newborn has a cap on, but there is very good reason for this. It's important that we provide plenty of warmth to our children during their first seven years of development. Normally we are told to dress our children as we would ourselves, or to simply touch their skin and see if they are warm to the touch. At first I thought this was valuable advice. After all, when I learned it I was a new mom and trusted every piece of expert advice my pediatrician offered.

Later, I learned that it wasn't exactly that simple. After all, why would my wardrobe, or that of any adult, be sufficient for a newborn child. My skin is completely different from that of a newborn, and a baby is much more sensitive. He cannot regulate his own temperature yet, and my idea of warmth is very different from a newborn's. Let's not forget to mention the hormonal imbalance right after birth that contributes to hot flashes and erratic body temperature for all new moms—and any other condition that contributes to the imbalance in body temperature that mothers experience.

Today, I have the courage to say that I do not agree with my pediatrician's advice, nor do I really need anyone to tell me that an adult's need for warmth is different from that of a newborn or a child.

After sifting through a few pediatric articles and opinions, I found one that sided with my bias, written by Susan R. Johnson, MD, FAAP.[6] She explains that if a child is wet or cold, it is then using its potential "growth" energy to heat its body. This energy would be "better utilized in further developing their brain, heart, liver, lungs and other organs," instead of creating heat. Therefore, if we use organic cotton or wool (see Resources)

---

[6]   "The Importance of Warmth", 2/11/2000, www.youandyourchildshealth.org.

to insulate their little bodies, then their "growth" energy can be used to develop healthy little children as was intended.

How often did we, as children, hear our mothers tell us to always be warm and dry, otherwise we would catch a cold? The reason is that if our bodies use valuable energy to create heat, then there is not enough energy to fight off any bugs or viruses with which we come in contact. Wetness and cold simply suppress the immune system of any human.

My chiropractor suggested that my infant's scully would help with relieving his acid reflux. He explained that all development is taking place in the brain, and therefore the head should always be covered. (Both of my children were baldies for their first year, and so a year-round scully was a good little head cover.) If the brain is not chilled, then it uses its energy to help develop all organs and systems. Since the digestive system would not be fully developed until around the seventh month, it was important that I did my part to keep his head warm to help his brain use its energy for proper digestive development. This could decrease the discomfort caused by an undeveloped digestive system. Later, a naturopath confirmed that in Eastern medicine, it is believed that a cold passes through the back of the lower head, and it is important to keep the head covered and warm. As an exhausted, desperate new mother, I kept a light cotton scully on my son's head for the whole summer, and then the whole year. Both my children now seek the comfort of their hat as it begins to cool even slightly.

Easy Ways to Keep Children Warm

So let's keep our children warm by insulating them with a layer of cotton, silk, or wool. Then dress them with their daily trendy outfit. And always layer. If it's cool out, put on a light hooded jacket, or at least keep it handy. This way if it gets cooler or warmer, you have options. If it's raining or snowing, then of course dress them in full rain and snow gear. For extreme cold, I would put on a wool hat beneath my kid's scully as well. I would use mittens instead of gloves, since the fingers are together in a mitten and can share their body heat to keep the other fingers warm. I suggest wool, silk, or cotton because these fabrics actually breathe, whereas synthetic fabrics (typically) do not. If your child is wearing polyester, for example, he may end up sweating. Because polyester doesn't breathe the way organic fabrics do, the sweat is then trapped against his body, thus causing him to be chilled and wet instead of dry when he cools down.

Holding, Carrying, and "Wearing" our Babies

So here began the backbreaking holding ritual that was one of the most loving experiences that both my children and I ever had. Like I said earlier, from the very beginning, my son made it very clear that he never wanted to be alone—he did not want to be put down for more than a few minutes, or to sleep alone. Basically, he wanted me 24/7, and I did not know how to handle this. I found myself stuck at home during the summer—the first three months of his little life. Here's what I did to keep life calm and simple.

Baby Slings Make it Much Better

Don't wait as long as I did to take action and figure out a resolution. No need to stay home if you'd rather not. Find what works for you. Since it was my first go at this, I didn't realize how many options I had or how to make it easier to hold my child. At the time I had no like-minded friends to ask for advice—not that I even knew what kind of "minded" parent I was or what category exactly I fit into. I quickly began looking for alternative methods for nursing and holding in books and on the Internet. I wanted to begin living a life again but I did not want to let go of my baby. I ordered my first sling (since he hated the Bjorn), and tried that. It was the Maya sling. Just looking at this sling was intimidating at first, and so I hung it over my headboard as decoration for the first few weeks. And instead of using a carrier, I began just walking around the block and simply holding my son in my arms so that we could get some fresh air.

Community Can Make all the Difference

I then found a local La Leche League (LLL), which was a nightmare to drive to, since my son wailed the entire car ride. He and my daughter both had motion sickness. Drained and hopeless, I arrived with my Maya sling and was hesitant to even share about my horrible parenting experience, since I was sure that I was a failure. Within minutes, I heard story after story about similar situations, and even more demanding ones. I could barely believe that so many people had similar challenging experiences after giving birth—how was it possible for all of these women to remain sane after being spread so thin?

I learned from my community that it does get better, and I would eventually see the light of day more often. It was suggested that I meditate and envision it happening. I also got some great advice while talking to one mom from the LLL about her similar experience. She struck a cord with me when she said that before too long my son would want more than just mommy. She reassured me, he would *want* to explore the world beyond our safe little cocoon, but for now I was his whole world, as I should be. This may or not be typical, but if you're having difficulty, always remember to reach out to like-minded individuals for support, comfort and feedback. It will keep you from feeling isolated or feeling like you're the only one who ever had this problem. And that will make all the difference.

Needless to say, support and community is crucial, especially for beginner parents. By the end of the meeting, with the help of my new mommy friends, I had a very calm and content son in my sling, I was walking around with my hands free, and I was actually able to hold adult conversations. I was grateful for the much-needed feedback and advice. From that moment, I made sure to surround myself one way or another with a supportive, like-minded community—whether through blogging, park friends, mommy and me programs, or whatever, and to always hold my baby just as he wanted to be held.

Eventually, I learned to nurse with my baby in my sling, while I walked and shopped, washed dishes, or went to dinner. Plus, my son loved being outdoors, and this became something new we could do together and both enjoy. Little by little, I began to get some normalcy in my life again. I also began to trust myself and to feel more confident in my parenting abilities.

My bond with my son grew more and more with each day, as we began to enjoy new experiences together.

Growing Out of the Holding Phase

Parents, I promise you that you will not be required to hold your baby forever—nor will he want you to. The "Velcro baby," constant-holding phase will pass. This period is so short-lived… and as challenging and backbreaking as it seems at times, try to enjoy it because it lasts as long as a blink of an eye. By the time the baby reaches toddler years, he no longer wants to be attached to you. This evolves into more of "checking in," and then off they go exploring again. Actually, the stronger your bond and the more secure your child grows from your constant connection in the early weeks, the better your chances are of raising an independent and confident child. He will know that you will be there for him if he needs you. And when it's time to venture off for a few minutes, he will not be afraid or worried.

My children are considered to be very independent, social, and confident by their teachers, friends, and many others. Their inner focus, confidence, and centeredness is clear, and there is no ambivalence in their daily actions. They are pretty well grounded and solid throughout their day. They are aware of how good their world is, how secure they are, what boundaries they have, and yet how free they are to safely explore. Know that this holding phase is an investment for your children and your future relationships with them. During a challenging moment, remind yourself to try to enjoy your baby's breathing, sounds, smell, and love. They will only want to be stuck to you for a short while, relatively speaking, and soon they will be off on their own journey.

Baby-Wearing our Children Throughout Time

Some encouraging information that helped me during my challenging moments came from reading that, although our culture is changing, our evolutionary need for skin-to-skin contact remains the same. We were born to be carried by our mothers, and our brain is still in desperate need of it, as our own proper development to parenthood depends on it. Many studies have been done on cultures where women still wear their babies for most of the day. These have shown that babies who are carried like this are more likely to have healthy pelvises, hips, and spines, as well as stronger respiratory systems when compared to babies who were not "worn" by their mothers all day. Another result is a strong bond between mother and child, and a very happy, alert baby, which is worth the investment. Parents today are lucky to have many wonderful baby carrier options available to them. Please check the Resources section or my website for the information on where you can find them.

I believe wearing the baby works better than anything else. If your baby is crying or fussing, and you hold him, jiggle him, and sing to him—he hears your heart, feels your warmth, smells his mommy, is able to nurse easily, and the world is a beautiful place. It became much easier to parent when I began wearing my baby, and I know that my son became more trusting of me and his world.

As you begin wearing your baby often, you will surely get the well-intended advice from loved ones not to carry your baby all the time or you will "spoil" him. Well, the fact is that you can't spoil a little baby who does not know how to take advantage of you. Your baby can only respond to its natural instincts for survival. His brain is not yet wired to manipulate you or his environment. He only wants to make sure his needs are met. So if your baby is crying, whether the reason seems minor or huge, it is important that mommy or someone who loves and cares for him is there to comfort and hold him at that moment.

The Science Behind It

In case you want scientific evidence to prove this to your mom and friends, the following is a great study to report. The Institute of Hearth Math conducted numerous studies through the years on the little brain in your chest called your heart (www.heartmath.org). It's worth looking further into these studies, but for now I will simply explain something wonderful that they discovered.

Various people were tested in groups of two. Their ages varied, as did the relationships between the two subjects. During the test, they stood next to each other, and their heart waves (ECG, echocardiogram frequencies) and brain waves (EEG, electroencephalogram frequencies) were recorded. The Institute reported that when the two human beings were near each other, their heart waves and their brain waves actually began to form the same wave pattern after a few minutes, meaning that the waves from their own hearts and brain were now in harmony within themselves *and* with each other. (Originally neither of the waves were in sync.) Then, the Institute had the two individuals make physical contact. The study reported that if there is physical contact between the two people, the wavelength increases, and it still flows at the same rate between the two of them. That is a beautiful, harmonious connection.

In lay terms, your heart and brain waves can affect another person's heart and brain waves. One's emotional energy registers in another's, and one person's heart waves affects another's heart and brain, for wonderful heart-brain synchronization. The study states:

> Our mental and emotional state impacts the quality of contact we offer to another person. When we touch one another with safe, respectful, loving intention both physically and emotionally, we call into play the full healing power of the heart. The greater the "coherence"—a sense that life is comprehensible, manageable and meaningful—one develops, the more sensitive one becomes to the subtle electromagnetic signals communicated by those around them. [7]
>
> How beautiful is that?

Normally this coherence and synchronization is not the case. A person's individual brain waves and heart waves don't normally flow at the same rate, and of course they do not flow at the same rate as our neighbor's. When we have contact, though, in some magical, mysterious way, there is harmony. We are connected beings. And so our connections are sometimes deeper

---

[7]   See Children, Doc and Howard Martin, *The HeartMath Solution: The Institute of HeartMath's Revolutionary Program for Engaging the Power of the Heart's Intelligence*, New York: HarperCollins Publishers (1999).

than we realize—for synchronicity on a physical, emotional, and spiritual level. As people and as parents, if we can practice being conscious of this reality, we will essentially be practicing wholistic parenting and living.

Another great study I found is the Harvard Mastery Stress Test, where about 200 male Harvard medical students were studied to determine how much parental nurturing they experienced during their infant and childhood years. These men were placed into two groups, those who received adequate nurturing and those who did not. After forty years, these same men were given physical examinations. In the group where the men stated that they were supported and well nurtured, approximately 25 percent of them experienced age-related illnesses. In the other group, where the men said that they lacked adequate parental nurturing, 89 percent of them suffered from age-related illnesses.[8]

Later, two scientists from the University of Arizona, Gary Schwartz and Linda Russek,[9] further tested a representative group of these same men by wiring them for EEG (brain) and ECG (heart) frequencies. Their study further revealed how the immune systems and emotional systems are directly related to early nurturing. The men with less parental nurturing during childhood experienced more illness in their later years. And so, based on this study, we can see that how well we nurture our children can directly affect their immunity, health, and emotional state of being— during infancy and throughout their lives.

Emotional deprivation during infancy and childhood may predispose a human being to a lifetime of disease, not to mention the emotional and psychological side effects due to loneliness and isolation.

I write this not just from my own experience of how juicy and wonderful it is to hold your child. There is actual scientific evidence available to us, which encourages us to do so. It is now time to be guided by our loving hearts and provide our children with all the nurturing that we can. And this is really simple and easy to do. A constant cuddly hug can't be all that challenging to give, can it? Enjoy it. It's good for your health as well.

[8]   Daily News (Los Angeles, CA), Mar 20, 1996, "Children Who Feel Loved Grow to Be Healthy Adults, Study Finds."

[9]   *Ibid.*

Meditation

Find a quiet moment. That quiet peaceful moment may only exist during a nursing session. Close your eyes and take a few deep breaths. Begin visualizing yourself and your baby connected (via any sort of carrying option). See the two of you smiling and enjoying the love that is flowing between both of you. See the golden light of love exchanged between your heart and your child's. There is nothing greater, better, more healing and more bonding than that moment. Know that this will last you a lifetime. Your connection is forever. Experience the magnitude of that exchange and connection. Let it run through your entire body and your child's. Open your eyes. Enjoy.

CHAPTER 12

Breastfeeding

B y now, it's safe to assume that most parents understand the significance of holding off on formula, or possibly not giving any formula at all. The synthetic substitute for breast milk simply does not compare to what nature has gifted to every mammalian creature on our planet. When I read "A Call to Action on Breastfeeding" from our Surgeon General published on January 2011, I realized that even "the powers that be" are now aware of how crucial nursing is. However, this statement caused me to worry: If there is a need for a call for action by the government, there must not be as many mothers in our country who are nursing their children as there should be. In fact, there are not. While 75 percent of U.S. babies start out breastfeeding, the Centers for Disease Control and Prevention says that only 13 percent are exclusively breastfed at the end of six months. Wow, mamas, I do believe we can do better than that, even without a call to action! What we need is a little support, information, and restructuring in the home and in the country when it comes to our view on breastfeeding.

The Basic Benefits of Breastfeeding

Let's begin with some simple reasons why this is so important—such as that breast milk is the only stuff on earth that has natural disease-fighting antibodies that help protect our babies from illnesses. Should a little illness come on, breast milk is the only substance your child can really take in. I remember when my son had a stomach virus. His pediatrician was happy to hear that I was still nursing, because that was the only liquid he could really recommend to help my son's little body get over the virus while also keeping him hydrated. If I hadn't been nursing, he would have followed his protocol and suggested Pedialyte to help with hydration. Given the choice, I preferred to avoid all the sugars and unpleasant taste of Pedialyte and stick to my milk.

Nursing was not just hydrating my baby, it was also serving as an antibiotic—which kept us out of the Emergency Room (ER). In the event that I wasn't nursing, I still would not have given my child anything synthetic like Pedialyte, when there are excellent alternatives available. The reality is that neither of my children has ever been to the ER for any reason at all yet. The only time my son ever saw the inside of a hospital was when I gave birth to his little sister. This has a lot to do with the healthy nurturing they have been consuming since the day that they were born.

I needn't mention that the more you nurse, the less likely it is that your children will be affected by whatever bugs are going around anyway. Studies show that there is also a lower risk of SIDS, obesity, allergies, leukemia, respiratory infections, and diabetes among children who nurse. Breast milk also boosts intelligence for baby, and

> Organic, raw coconut water has the same five essential electrolytes as breast milk: calcium, potassium, phosphorus, magnesium, and sodium. It has 15 times more potassium than most sports drinks on the market. And it doesn't have anything artificial in it at all, making it a perfect electrolyte rehydrating drink, and a healthier alternative to Pedialyte.

the list of advantages is long. Check out the La Leche League's website, **www. llli.org,** for the rest of this list and for support groups to get you through.

Mom's health also benefits, as her chance for breast cancer and ovarian cancer decreases dramatically. Because it raises oxytocin, a "happy" hormone, breast feeding also reduces stress levels and the risk of postpartum depression. Mothers often claim feelings of euphoria during a nursing session, and I can attest to that.

And since nature provided us with this magical milk for our babies, we can be thankful that it also helps keep our expenses low when it comes to medical bills, helping us save on antibiotics and expensive formulas. The more we nurse, the more we also save financially.

Of course, there is also the beautiful, magical bonding during breast feeding that nothing else compares to. I have yet to meet a mother who could tell me she did not truly enjoy the bonding part of nursing—no matter how challenging nursing may have been for her.

Heart Synchronization

Once mom and baby have smoothed out whatever problems may have occurred when the baby first started nursing, there is a major exchange of hormones and energy between the two of them. It's not just a passing of fluids from one person to another. The baby is actually ingesting life from his mother, and is connected to her from the area near her heart. There is a deeper connection taking place, as studies at the Institute of Heart Math have proven. Since it is true, as we have described, that the brain waves and heartbeat of two individuals come into sync on contact, mommy and baby are completely in tune with each other during nursing and are connected energetically, emotionally, and physically. Can anyone imagine anything more magical? There is no deeper, more loving connection between mother and child than in that nursing moment.

Before considering formula for your child, please make sure you look into all your options. An informed choice can really make a difference in your child's health. In addition to the synthetic material that your child will consume, many formula products contain aluminum, which is a known cancer-causing ingredient. Add to this the fact that the three major formula companies, Similac, Enfamil and Nestle Good Start, all contain Genetically Modified Organisms (GMOs) in their formula. GMOs have been shown to cause birth defects, cancer, organ failure, leaky gut syndrome, and other major health issues. If you have no other choice, an organic formula would be a healthier option than a non-organic one, because organic formulas do not have GMOs in them.

Inner Knowing Is Empowering

So I repeat: There needs to be some rewiring of our thinking when it comes to something so important, coming not only from our government and the corporate world supporting and encouraging us, but from our homes. Or better yet, when it comes to nursing, maybe if we just tap in to our inner wisdom a little bit more, instead of giving in or listening to all that is said "out there," then we will be guided in the direction we need to go as a family unit, and the direction we have always taken as a species.

If you look around, you will notice that no other animal needs milk from another species or parenting direction from a book, an expert, or the Internet. You can, however, notice in our intuitive birthing and parenting as humans, an inner knowing of how to raise the younger generation. You can also notice this in communities of other species, such as primates. My point is that we need to go back to our true nature when it comes to parenting skills like nursing. We already have thousands, if not millions of years of "knowing." It's there in us. Sure, a little reminder and support can help, but at the deepest level of our being, we already know how to do things like breastfeed and raise a child. If you want to tap into this deep knowledge, just take a few deep breaths and tap into an ancient intelligence that is imprinted within every part of you.

I think about how far we have strayed from our true nature when a culture believes that it is okay and natural to drink the milk of another animal, but it may not be acceptable in some instances for a baby to actually drink its own mother's milk. Seriously, what happened there? When was the last time you saw an infant monkey nursing from a cow? Occasionally I will come across something in the media about a mom being penalized for nursing her child in public. Something seems so wrong about *that*. As a society, we should never penalize mothers for nursing their children with our own species' milk supply or motivate them to feed their children milk from another species—especially if the reason is considered to be public indecency.

Can Dads Nurse?

This section wouldn't be complete without my sharing how crucial a partner's role is in breastfeeding. Honestly, the support of a father or partner is what determines the success and length of this God-given process. A family should never underestimate the importance of a partner's presence, love, support, and involvement with his family. What research has shown is that generally, if a partner is not as committed to breastfeeding as a mother is, the long-term success of breastfeeding is affected. Ultimately, the mother is left alone and is not as supported to nurse, which may leave her feeling overwhelmed, isolated, and resentful. And during those challenging moments, she may feel like throwing up her hands and quitting all together. If she has a partner to support and nurture her during her difficult times, she will endure, which allows the entire family to benefit from the breastfeeding experience.

In the instance where a mother may or may not be experiencing difficulty with her breastfeeding, but her partner is resentful of it, this causes strain in her relationship, and this too will ultimately negatively affect how long she will nurse her baby.

However, when the partner is involved, and breastfeeding is of the utmost importance for the family, research has shown that the entire dynamic and energy of the unit is benefitted. During mom's hard times, dad is there to help, encourage, love, and support both his wife and child. During mom's blissful nursing moments, dad is there to also enjoy the experience and to rest assured that his child is enjoying the best things life can offer at this time. And through these experiences, studies reveal that the benefits of breastfeeding are more healthy and long-lasting.

It May Not Always Be So Blissful

When it came to breastfeeding, I thought I was golden. At the hospital, my milk came in the morning after delivery; my son latched on nicely, and drank away like a champ. I looked forward to our next feeding session. I could not get enough of it—wow, I had no idea how beautiful this experience was. I was so in love with my son, our nursing, our immediate bond, and the whole new parent feeling. It was all heavenly. My room actually felt like heaven, and my son was truly the angel blessing it. I was so happy that I would find myself crying about it throughout the day.

Then when we arrived home, my breastfeeding experience took a sudden unexpected turn. We came home to a tremendous amount of external stressors, which we were foolish enough to allow into our life.

This immediately began affecting and slowing down my milk supply. By the second week, my son had acid reflux, which caused me to eliminate absolutely all dairy and dairy proteins (like casein) from my diet. Dairy is particularly associated with reflux, as are wheat, soy, peanuts, spices, caffeine, and eggs. I will say more on how we treated this later.

In addition to the reflux, my son was also a ravenous nurser. At first, my milk supply couldn't keep up with his demand. I tried visualizations to get me through this time. I would relax, take deep breaths, and envision a waterfall of milk, and that always helped me have a "let down." Of course, this would be quite the task if my son was screaming at the top of his lungs for his milk. He nursed all day and night, every half hour to an hour. He also comfort nursed in between.

Within the first few months, although my supply had calibrated to his needs, I began experiencing mastitis, nipple blanching, and stretched out nipples like no one had ever seen before, constant leaking, and many other complications. I couldn't pump, since it was so painful. He also enjoyed one breast more than the other for comfort reasons, and so I had one boob that was two sizes larger than the other. This beautiful experience had become a nightmare.

Throughout this time, my husband attempted desperately to contact everyone and anyone who could guide us through this rough time. We contacted the hospital's lactation consultant (who called us back only once), local La Leche League moms, who were so helpful and a true blessing for our family, books (*The Breastfeeding Book* by Dr. Sears is one I love), our pediatrician, Internet blogs, chat groups, and eventually I attended a local La Leche League group.

My poor husband would skim through books for me, browse the Internet, and call various people, trying to explain the situation while I attempted to calm our baby. You name it, he was there for us. He would encourage me verbally, physically, mentally, spiritually, and in any other way you can imagine. And during the times that I would say, "That's it, tomorrow I'm giving him the formula," or "I think this is my last week of nursing," he would always respond by saying, "Okay, just wait until then to see how you feel, and I trust your decision. Everything will be fine either way." This unconditional support is what helped me through all of our breastfeeding struggles.

It Gets Better

When my son was five months, most of my breastfeeding issues had smoothed out. What I found was that when my son began sleeping in his own crib, he nursed significantly less. By the time he was nine months, he suddenly did not want to nurse from me anymore, and preferred the bottle. One night, I had his bottle filled and placed on the floor next to me (as backup), while I was nursing him in his dark room. He pulled away from me over and over again. I then gave him the bottle, and he drank the entire thing. I was definitely heartbroken. There is an emptiness that you may feel when you know that your time to nurse is about over. Because I was never able to pump, my milk supply decreased, until one day I was completely dried up.

I ended up giving him the best formula that I could find for him at the time, one that would be organic, gentle on his tummy, and not ignite his reflux. He was on it for two short months, and I then quickly began giving him organic goat's milk instead.

Get the Support You Need

As far as community and reaching out goes, the La Leche League helped out in the beginning. Many moms in my community are very grateful to the Holistic Moms Network, because it really guided them through all their challenges. Dr. Sear's *Breastfeeding Book* is a good book to read before the baby arrives, and gave me the information that I needed to start nursing. Nowadays there are also blogs like mine (www.lovecenteredparenting.com) that you can chat and share on. By the time my daughter came around, I was surrounded by like-minded friends, and we were nursing during play dates, in public, in school, and we never thought twice about it, since this is what we all did. Any issues were discussed during a nursing session and stories were shared that made it more comforting.

With my daughter, from day one I knew what to expect and what to do when it came to nursing. I knew how to hold her, how to not let her nurse herself to sleep, how to anoint my nipples with products that protected them, how to calibrate my supply, and really just how to enjoy it from the very beginning. She was colicky, and I had to tweak my diet once again. A dear friend introduced me to therapeutic grade essential oils by Young Living during that time, and I began using these miraculous oils for her colic and sleep issues, which thankfully helped her significantly. I was able to nurse her for 15 months, until I eventually weaned her due to sleep issues. She then began drinking raw cow's milk. She never went on formula, and I feel grateful for that, because I feel like it really served her little body well.

I will end here by sharing probably the most important piece of information of the chapter. Like I said, it's become pretty clear that nursing is something that we should all seriously consider; as we become more aware of the benefits we can communicate this awareness to our families, coworkers, communities, and the nation. Let's share this message and information with any new parent who is struggling, and let's support them. All that being said, we need to remember that any breastfeeding is better than none. And so if you decide that this is not something that you can do much longer and the stress is outweighing the benefits, then by all means do what you intuitively feel is best for you, your baby, and your family. And I will repeat: No one knows this better than mom.

Meditation for Nursing Challenges

Close your eyes, take a few deep breaths and relax. If your baby is screaming during this moment, know that your child is okay and held by you, and has all the love he needs. Your milk is on its way now. See an enormous waterfall flowing with milk. It is abundantly flowing down into a stream. The flow is endless and strong. You and your baby can drink some of this milk. Continue to see it flow, flow, flow. It's here. Slowly come back and try to get your baby to latch on, so that the baby can also stimulate your supply. Chances are if you're relaxed, the baby will relax as a result of your calmer energy and also latch on better.

You can also affirm every morning that you have an abundant, healthy supply of milk. Affirm this constantly throughout your day for the first six to eight weeks.

CHAPTER 13

Healthy Diet

I'm sure you have guessed that my fertility struggles not only shaped my diet, but my entire family's menu as well. We quickly realized that you are only as healthy as what you put into your body. If you want a healthy life, healthy immune system, and healthy future for your child, you must start by eating in a healthy way prior to conception, into pregnancy, and finally from infancy until the day your growing teenagers simply request that you lay off them and let them pick their own food. Chances are that even if you're told to "buzz off" by a rebellious teenager, he will later come back to his culinary roots as soon as the adolescent haze clears.

Healthy Body Prior to Conception

I just want to briefly mention again how important it is to prepare our bodies prior to conception for the beautiful experience of pregnancy. This is a practice that many traditional cultures throughout the world have passed along through the generations. In fact, Weston A. Price noted during his worldwide investigations of indigenous people that when a couple was contemplating having a child, there was a period of special feeding before conception, for *both* parents. Their family would assist them in providing nutrient-dense animal foods, and this specific diet would continue into healthy pregnancy, lactation, and the raising of healthy children. Tribes from Canada, Florida, Australia, New Zealand, the Amazon, Peru, and

Africa stuck to their nourishing traditional diets, and did not take in any industrialized, refined, or denatured food like refined sugar, white flour, canned foods, high fructose corn syrup, refined or hydrogenated vegetable oils, colorings, additives, or other toxic ingredients. They also consumed raw milk, lots of lard, butter, coconut, palm and palm kernel oils, and ate a lot of fish liver oils, such as cod liver oil. Their diets naturally had equal amounts of omega-6 and omega-3 essential fatty acids. Dr. Price was a dentist, and so he first observed and noted that for the most part indigenous people's teeth and jaw lines were healthy, free of decay, they had a positive and happy outlook on life, and had strong immune systems with no childhood illness, and virtually a disease-free life.

I think there's something that can be learned from what has happened in our disease-ridden, obesity-prone culture, which has long abandoned its traditional diet. Unfortunately, annual statistics show that our country's diet is quite poor, and our people have a vast number of health issues due to obesity and poor diet. Yet, this is what the majority of the U.S. culture has endorsed, and the consequence of disease is not beneficial to anyone. When we eat fast foods, processed food, genetically modified food, and chemically-laden food, our bodies are receiving no nutritional value from our food. We are starving our bodies of nutrition, while we are feeding it more calories than it could ever need—and these calories are loaded with chemicals and toxins. I know that the state of our health and that of our children is suffering. So please be mindful of what you are feeding yourself and your children, because you are creating health standards for our future generations. Educate yourself about this subject, and always check the sources of your information. The truth is always out there—we simply need to weed through what's available to find it.

If you are ready to make a change, start by slowly introducing better options, such as a plant-based diet, and mostly organic, non-GMO, unprocessed, fresh and local food. In other words, real unprocessed food. Once your body receives real nutrition from real food, you will slowly begin to see a difference in your overall health. You can do this in baby steps; try it for 10 days and then if you like the results, go for another 10 days and keep going from there, and see where you end up. Who knows, maybe this change will be a life-altering event.

As you may remember, before conceiving our son, my diet included whole food supplements, which I also took during my pregnancy, a daily intake of Greens First, and mostly whole, organic food. I also stayed away from processed foods, such as cold cuts, too many sweets, fried foods, and whatever logically seemed unhealthy. I did enjoy being a glutton during my last trimester. However, although I ate large amounts of food, I had healthy cravings for the most part. I was absolutely in love with peanut butter and jelly sandwiches from conception to delivery, and organic eggs were second on that list. So munch away, but eat consciously, because whatever you're indulging in, so is your little baby. Louise Hay once wrote, "If it doesn't grow, don't eat it." I would say this is a simple rule to keep in mind when you're making your grocery list.

In case you are binging on junk food and can't seem to help yourself (it happens!), you may need some information to understand how what you eat during pregnancy will affect your child for the rest of its life. A new research report published online in *The FASEB Journal* suggests that pregnant mothers whose diets are high in sugar and fat have babies who are likely to become junk-food junkies themselves.[10] According to the report, based on a study using rats, this happens because the high fat and sugar diet leads to changes in the fetal brain's reward pathways, altering food preferences. And so this study shows how it is possible for a child to have a preference for junk food over healthy food even from before birth, as a result of mom's diet during pregnancy.

So, if you're having a serious craving during pregnancy for something unhealthy, you could try a good mantra or affirmation to help rewire your thoughts. Affirmations not only help with rewiring of brain patterns, but, over time, they slowly allow less and less room for the negative thought, as the positive one takes over. If you're having a need to eat unhealthy food, try repeating something like, "I release the need to eat unhealthy foods," or maybe, "I love and honor my body and my baby." Do this a few times a day in front of the mirror while looking straight into your own eyes, and say it with feeling. The results may surprise you and motivate you to invite affirmations into other parts of your life for some overall healing. Louise

---

[10] Nathan Gray, "Pre-pregnancy diet may be just as important as material diet, study suggests," www.nutraingredients.com, 9/24/12, reporting on a study by Dr. Mikhail Niculescu.

Hay is the pioneer of affirmations—see her books and website at www. louisehay.com if you need to "clean house" prior to your baby's arrival.

Healthy Diet for Baby

When the baby finally arrives, as I've mentioned before, breast milk is the only food your baby should consume. Experts now agree that you should breastfeed for almost the entire first year—at least seven to nine months before introducing formula. Recently, more and more doctors have agreed that the longer you hold off on solids, the more beneficial it is for your child. This helps prevent food allergies, diabetes, and other ailments. I know how eagerly I waited for my son to eat his first meal. Back then, his first meal was a boiled organic apple. Nowadays there's more information as to what the sequence should be when introducing solids, to be more aligned with the digestive system's development.

Parents, please know that if you do the best you can, and feed your little ones as nature intended, their digestive systems will continue to strengthen and mature by the time they are six years old. And if you maintain a healthy diet, as well as keeping other harmful environmental factors at a minimum, their digestive systems will strengthen even more throughout their lives.

Various schools of medicine throughout the world state that the overall health of infants and children correlates with the strength and health of their digestive systems. A healthy digestive lining means a healthy immune system—and this goes for everyone, but especially for children. Because of their immature digestive systems, children will need a different food menu to allow their systems to mature. So, no steaks for them any time soon.

Always keep in mind that a healthy diet and lifestyle mean a healthy child. This will become evident rather quickly, if they suddenly become weaker or get sicker more often. If our children do become sick, we can work on getting their diet back on track, and we can always visit a chiropractor or acupuncturist in order to help speed up their recovery and rebalance their systems.

A Gentle Approach to Food

As a rule, it is suggested that parents simply wait to feed their little ones solid foods at least until their teeth are in, since chewing is the first and most important step in the digestion process. Without it, the unchewed food will go into their belly like rocks. They will not be able to digest their food well until they can break it down somewhat through chewing, which means they will not absorb all the nutrients in their food until they can chew. So you're better off sticking with your breast milk, if the little teeth haven't made their way through. Other factors to keep in mind, which show that she is ready, are that your child is able to sit up on her own, has lost the tongue-thrusting and gag reflexes when foods are put in her mouth, is able to pick up food and put in it in her mouth, and she grabs at and shows interest in your food. Your maternal instincts (and not your neighbor's or well-meaning mother's) will tell you that your child is ready.

When you begin to make food for your children, always cook it at a low temperature, as you would when baking and roasting. I always boiled my children's food and then pureed it, since they didn't have many teeth to chew with yet. Try to feed them food that is in season and in harmony with nature. Start with the green veggies first, such as summer squash, green beans, and avocado. Then slowly add all the orange veggies, like carrots and sweet potatoes. Carrots, spinach, beets, turnips, or collards are too rich in nitrates for a baby until he is at least nine months old. You can also incorporate herbs in their meals, which are wonderful and therapeutic, in case you did cheat a bit and give your child something like a banana, for example. Bananas cause mucous in the belly, and the herbs will aid the digestive lining in eliminating the thick, damp layer of mucous that the banana left behind.

About a month after you've watched your little child enjoy all this new, yummy food, you can begin giving cooked fruits, like applesauce, peaches, apricots, pears, nectarines, and plums. Once they've reached at least nine months old, add other steamed or raw veggies like zucchini, broccoli, cauliflower, tomatoes, spinach, beets, and collard greens. You can add the legumes after a year, and by then you can also add eggs, too. A few months after, I personally introduced wild, low-mercury fish and organic chicken, and a small amount of grass-fed organic beef. Until this day, my children hardly ever eat red meat. They like their healthy food, because it's what they know. And even when we do go to birthday parties that have pizza and cake, they dive in for these goodies at first, but then leave half of them behind. They are not the biggest junk food eaters—although they do believe they are fans. As I type this, my son has an enormous bag filled with chocolate and candy from a piñata he broke at a party. It's been sitting in his closet day after day and he still hasn't gone in to eat from it. So I say stick to your good diet, and chances are it will pay off.

To get you started, I recommend *Nourishing Traditions: The Cookbook that Challenges Politically Correct Nutrition and the Diet Dictocrats*, both excellent books by Sally Fallon that are based on Weston A. Price's diet. I would strongly recommend that you join Weston Price's website as well, at **www.westonaprice.org**, for all the valuable information that's shared there.

Food Sources

You should also keep in mind a few simple things mentioned by Michael Gaeta, my acupuncturist. Dr. Gaeta recommends a diet made up of whole foods and supplements, preferably organic and locally grown (which saves on energy to transport it), and eating "seasonal, fresh, with

Overall, I would stay away from the baby cereals, even if they are organic, and rice and soy products. Many doctors are no longer suggesting you start children with cereal, due to the many allergies which have arisen from wheat gluten. Soy products are highly controversial, and from what I have researched, the verdict is still not in. Like gluten, soy is also a common allergen. In that case, I would rather steer clear of something if it's not definitely known to be beneficial to my child. Why take the risk?

As for dairy, if it is pasteurized, there's really no health benefit to it. Everything added after the pasteurization process (heating and killing of everything in it) is synthetic anyway, so why add synthetics to our baby's diet? The FDA approves of raw cheese that has been aged for 60 days, so you may want to consider that.

Don't eliminate fat from your children's diet.

Finally, steer clear of basically any food that's white, like white rice, flour, wheat, salt, and sugar. Sugar is now known to be more addictive than cocaine, something to ponder when considering giving your child that cotton candy.

a balance of raw and cooked foods." He recommends eating raw, organic dairy, and organic, pasture-fed meat, fish, beans (except for soy beans), and using filtered water, and high-quality oils like olive and coconut oil. In cold, damp weather you would eat more cooked foods, and in the summer more raw food. As a substitute for breast milk, which is of course the best, he recommends raw cow's milk and raw goat's milk, avoiding pasteurization, which destroys the enzymes.

Because the soil is depleted today and our food is mostly processed, he believes that supplementation is a must, preferably supplements made from whole foods, not synthetic vitamins. He recommends supplements from Standard Process—they grow their own food for their vitamins on organic land—and Best Western herbs made by MediHerbs, an Australian company.

So, giving your children some good, simple food, a few supplements, and a healthy environment can really provide an awesome world for them to grow up in. Again, just keep it simple, and stick to eating whatever your garden would grow if you had one. And if you do have one, by all means give those goodies to your baby. My daughter's godmother collects all her garden veggies and stores them in her freezer for months so her baby can enjoy them when the time is right.

Bon Appétit.

Blessing or Prayer

Before beginning a meal, take a moment to say grace or bless your food before it enters your body. You may want to light a candle first, as it sets the mood and captures the children's attention. Hold hands and choose what resonates most for you and your family.

We take turns throughout the week, where the children pick different songs from their school's meal blessings, or my husband and I pick our own. One of my favorites from the children's school is:

> Earth who gave us all this food,
> Sun who made it ripe and good,
> Dearest Earth and dearest Sun,

We will not forget what you have done.
Blessings on our dinner.

One that I choose at times is:
May this meal and all the Beings that brought it to us be blessed, and may it bless our bodies. Amen

(Sometimes we specifically thank the animal that we are eating for giving itself to us.)

CHAPTER 14

Wholistic Healthcare

"Everyone has a doctor in him or her; we just have to help it in its work. The natural healing force within each one of us is the greatest force in getting well."

Hippocrates

B ased on my experience, I have now come to believe that there is a great misunderstanding in allopathic medicine when it comes to our bodies and our health. One of the most obvious contrasts between homeopathic and allopathic healthcare is how a person is treated for disease. Allopathic doctors will usually see a patient for up to 20 minutes, and then prescribe medication to treat the ailment they believe to be causing their patient's problems (according the complaints the patient described or a test result). Let's not mention how long you waited to see that doctor prior to your quick conversation with him. You go back for a follow-up a week later, and take it from there. There really is no true inquiry about the cause of your illness or the reason for your visit.

During your first visit with a holistic doctor, you will spend at least an hour talking about all aspects of your life. Most holistic doctors ask that you fill out a long questionnaire (mine was 20 pages long), inquiring about your and your family's medical history. For example, what your last three meals were, what daily products you use, your overall diet, your occupation, what school your child goes to, how many words they speak, and what their last poop was like. Why is all that necessary? Because it's all related to the reason for your visit. Every single part of you and your life is directly related to what your body is suffering from. The doctor views you as a whole being.

So let's say you visited the holistic pediatrician because you believe your child has a stomach virus. The pediatrician will ask you if your child has been under any environmental stress recently (such as a jam-packed week full of activities), if he is watching a lot of television, if he has been eating unhealthy sugars or starches, whether the family is under distress, and basically about anything that could compromise a healthy immune system. Normally, even if a stomach virus is going around, when your child is wholistically healthy (in mind, body and spirit), his immune system—his body armor against germs—usually will not allow anything that could compromise the body to get through its defenses. And, if he does catch a bug, his healthy body will get rid of the virus quickly, causing only mild symptoms—it's even possible that no one would notice that he had a virus.

This brings me to the very core of wholistic parenting, the reason why I strongly feel that we need to nurture our children on all three levels, so that they can grow and develop in a beautiful, healthy way.

Since life is not perfect, we are often required to adapt. As we navigate the ups and downs that life has in store for us, it may be difficult to balance all three aspects of our being in the healthiest way–either for ourselves or our children. I once read that if a muscle doesn't meet resistance it will not grow, and the same goes for our mind, body and soul. And so during our challenging moments, we may get sick. When we get physically sick, there are plenty of ways to heal ourselves, which nature has prescribed and provided since the beginning time. I always tell my fellow mom friends to simply try the natural approach first, and *if all else fails,* then go for the pharmaceuticals. This is because the medications will simply cause or lead to other problems. Sure, their side effects can often be minimal and easy to handle, but what if they aren't? We now know that there have been infant deaths and complications due to many over-the-counter, "mild," approved medications. You will hear about this in the media every so often. So why risk it, especially if there are powerful options that will knock a virus out in less time than any over-the-counter medication and without the side effects and other complications?

Traditional Treatment Without Side Effects

I was blessed by having all four of my grandparents in my life. One pair lived right next door during all of my childhood. One of the many things they taught me indirectly was that in nature we have all that we need to heal ourselves. During my grandparents' time, the pharmaceutical industry barely existed, and the world heavily relied on natural resources. Life in general was more connected to nature's gifts back then, and detrimental ingredients, medications, and processed foods were rare. Because of this I believe that, in many ways, people were healthier a generation or two ago, and even prior to that.

My grandparents quickly learned which remedies (available from nature) could be used to heal specific ailments, and this knowledge was passed on to me. I remember that when I had a cold, I was always given a scoop of raw honey, lemon tea, and cut up garlic, along with soups. (I was also advised to get lots of rest.) Another example is we used tomato paste on burns.

Growing up, we ate a Mediterranean diet, which was loaded with healthy ingredients, with powerful antioxidants like oregano and thyme, as well as an abundance of other herbs, such as dill and parsley. Of course, don't forget healthy olive oil, seafood (such as sardines), loads of vegetable dishes with dark greens, and other great healthy foods, which are part of the typical Mediterranean diet.

I am grateful that my grandparents and parents handed down to me their wisdom and connection to nature. Here I am today, doing the same things and even more with my family—and I hope that my children take it even further.

A Few of My Own Tips

When our little ones come down with a bug, we simply keep a watchful eye so that it does not develop into something different or more serious. In addition, we ease our children's symptoms as much as we can. By treating their symptoms naturally, we are also weakening the virus and helping it leave in a faster and more bearable manner. When I was nursing, my daughter had her first runny nose at about a year old or so. I made sure I ate loads of garlic, kefir (probiotics), lemon, organic herbal teas and broths. Garlic is known to be antiviral and antibacterial; kefir is full of wonderful probiotic communities, which promote a healthy digestive system (a large part of our immunity has to do with healthy gut flora); lemon and kiwi are known for their vitamin C, herbal teas for all their beneficial effects, and broths for their ability to help flush out the virus and keep your little patient well-hydrated. All of this entered her system as well and helped her body process her cold easier.

Diet during a cold plays a huge role, since many foods can help rid us of a cold while others can feed it. Sugars will absolutely feed any bug. In fact, studies have shown that a small morsel of sugar will suppress the immune system for up to six hours. Just think of how many foods have sugar in them that you eat regularly or when you are sick. Avoid processed foods, fried heavy foods, and wheat gluten. Keep it light.

Holistic experts will agree that soups and veggies are the best for children with colds or ear infections. Garlic and olive oil heated together and then added via dropper into the ear works miracles for ear infections.

When my daughter got her first ear infection at age four, it came in with a roar. It actually punctured her ear drum and left a very large hole, accompanied by hearing loss. Although our very concerned back-up pediatrician gave me an antibiotic prescription to give to her, I decided not to let fear guide my choices. Instead, I used Young Living's Melrose, Thieves, and Helichrysum oils around and in the back of her ear. Within two weeks, the hole was sealed and her hearing was completely restored.

Organic chamomile and ginger via dropper for infants relieves acid reflux or colic. Digize by Young Living rubbed on the belly for constipated infants is truly a gift at desperate times.

For more remedies, you can visit my blog at <u>www.lovecenteredparenting.com</u> or simply research some remedies for yourself. Dr. Palevsky's website (www.drpalevsky.com) is another one to visit. He has very helpful tips on how to fight a cold naturally.

As I mentioned before, my absolutely favorite remedies for infants and children are Young Living's essential oils. I began to appreciate these essential oils so much that I wanted to share them with the world. There is a list of oil remedies for colds that simply knock out a cold in about 24 hours. Time and time again, I have witnessed times when the oils ease symptoms like nothing else I can imagine.

Young Living's Thieves and peppermint oil are two remedies every mother should have handy in her purse at all times. When my children simply did not want to take supplements, a little lathering of oil on the bottom of their feet was the perfect solution. When they were a little older, in addition to the oils, I also gave my children Standard Process supplements during a cold. However, during their infancy, I would consume the supplements they needed and my children would then ingest them through my breast milk. I used a few basic ones like Andrographis Complex, Calcium Lactate, Thymex, and Echinacea Purporea (the real deal echinacea).

If you use pure products such as the ones mentioned, you not only get rid of your child's cold in a short time, but you are also building their immunity in a way that creates a foundation of health for them. You are basically allowing the virus to run through their system and create immunity, while at the same time weakening the virus and eliminating it through natural means. As I mentioned, this is all without adding any toxicity from pharmaceuticals, and without compromising their bodies further. When the body is compromised by the foods and medicines we ingest, it can create a health issue that will surface shortly after the cold has gone.

I encourage you to take the time to learn about what pharmaceuticals do to our bodies, including why and how these man-made chemicals work, and what occurs as a result of taking them. At the very least, please read the inserts in the box that your pharmaceutical is packaged in, so that you can find out about the side effects of that drug. It will be well worth your time.

Do Not Let Fear Lead the Way

Don't get me wrong. I am not against pharmaceuticals, and I do believe that they have their place, if used properly and when necessary. Once, I felt that my son's cold was progressing and, because he had had a severe cough for two weeks, I was worried that he would develop a secondary infection like pneumonia. I had no choice but to meet with our last-resort pediatrician (since my holistic one was away), and when she heard my son's lungs, she immediately wanted to put him on antibiotics. She said his lungs were in really bad shape, and that he was having a lot of trouble breathing. Fear was my first reaction, and I almost gave in to using antibiotics for the first time, since I didn't want his condition to worsen.

Instead, I took a deep breath, and then explained to her that no one in my family has had any antibiotics for over a decade. I went on to say that Western medicine is not my first line of treatment for any ailment. This began a conversation, which went pretty well, except for the fact that she knew nothing about the alternative options I was suggesting we try. She responded by saying that if there was no improvement in the bronchial infection in five days, she would strongly suggest we put him on antibiotics. The only reason she agreed to this was that she trusted that there must be something I was doing right if my children were rarely sick and were able to recover without the use of pharmaceuticals—ever. I did take the prescription, just in case.

I went home and did everything I knew of to heal his lungs and cold. I also reached out to friends and did my research. I learned that the bronchial infection was viral and that antibiotics couldn't help my son anyway. So I needed to find a way to treat him. I used a combination of healing modalities such as oils, diet, acupuncture, acupressure, rest, low stimulation, hot compresses, supplements, and juicing. My boy was a trouper and did all of it. It was a lot of work and we had a 45-minute healing ritual with all these modalities every night before bed.

When we returned for the follow-up visit five days later, the doctor could not believe it. In fact, she told me she had never seen anything like it. "Go mama!" she said. My son's lungs had completely cleared up, and she said she didn't need to see him again. She also asked me what exactly I did, and when I explained the process to her she responded that she knew nothing about what I did, but was happy to see how well and how fast it worked. She seemed like she really trusted my knowledge of alternative healing modalities. She now does not get involved with how I treat my children. She simply tells me what she sees with her tools, and I go home to administer whatever remedies will work to my children. When we go for the follow-up appointments, there is profound evidence of just how wonderful these remedies, intuition, and intentions can be.

Build a Like-Minded Practitioner Network to Support Your Intuition

It is important to have a dialogue with the pediatrician you choose. If you decide to find a holistic practitioner, you can begin your quest by asking like-minded friends, Googling, or simply interviewing a few from your insurance plan. Decide which qualities are important to you in a health provider and begin the process from there. Whoever you decide on has to be willing to work together with you as a team, and not dictate how you care for your child. The communication needs to remain open. Come to an agreement as I did with the conventional doctor. Hold your ground and do not be afraid to question the doctor or simply explain how you plan to return your child to health. You are the parent, and you are the caregiver, and you know best. If your doctor is not willing to work with you, then you know where the door is, so you can meet and interview with another one.

As my pediatrician, Dr. Palevsky believes, "It is important to help parents access their knowledge and strengthen their confidences through their own experiences and intuition, thus supporting the idea that parents are the primary care providers for their children. Parents deserve to have access to a healing model of healthcare that reduces the use of ineffective and harmful drug treatments, and empowers them to build healthy, vibrant bodies and spirits in themselves and in their children." My pediatrician and I are on the same page, and this is why I chose him and am grateful for his presence in our lives.

And at the end of the day, when your children are sick, whether it is for the very first time or with something later on, try seeing their cold as a rite of passage for you and your child. It actually helps build your healing muscles, so that you can arm yourself with new tools and strengthen your feelings of empowerment.

Every time you help your child through an illness you will come to realize your parent-healing potential. You and your child begin to understand and grow in your faith in yourselves, each other, and Mother Earth. And if you find yourself in a scenario where you feel more comfortable reaching out to a practitioner, by all means do it! Allow yourself the opportunity to seek out help when needed. That is also a good practice in itself.

CHAPTER 15

Vaccination

"I will follow that regimen which, according to my ability and judgment, I consider for the benefit of my patients, and abstain from whatever is deleterious, and mischievous. I will give no deadly medicine to anyone if asked…"

Hippocratic Oath

E very time I read that part of the Hippocratic Oath, I wonder how many physicians are mindful of their oath during the course of their daily practice. I have not always found that these words of Hippocrates are being honored. This has been my experience and that of countless mothers in my community. When it comes to vaccines, I believe they do more harm than good. But because vaccinating our children is such an integral form of health care in our culture, many people do not question the safety or efficacy of vaccines. I feel compelled to share what I've learned, knowing that some of the information and statistics will be hard to believe at first. I will begin by suggesting that you try to remain open to it and know that it takes an openness to fairly evaluate this issue.

Life is full of decisions, big and small: what shoes to buy, what home to live in, what job to accept, what school your kids attend, which foods to eat. With that said, when it comes to vaccinating your children, I sincerely hope that you ask yourself very simple questions before making a major decision such as the one about vaccinations, you read up on the subject, and question your own beliefs. I believe that the decision should be made by you and your partner, not your doctor or society, that is, unless you have sincere religious beliefs on the subject. In this case, you don't really have to make the decision, because it has been made for you already. After making a well-informed and educated decision, the next step would be to pick your physician and have a conversation about your family's beliefs. Having a supportive, well informed and educated pediatrician that will support you and your concerns is the next largest choice to make. It is important to feel aligned with the person who will be collaborating with you for your child's well being.

My journey on vaccine research began with Dr. Sherri Tenpenny's DVD *Vaccines: The Risks, the Benefits, the Choices*. I have to admit that initially, I watched the DVD with much skepticism. I was definitely floored by the vast amount of information, some of it quite unsettling, that this DVD introduced me to. Because I was in shock and disbelief, I began to do my own research. I wanted to find something comforting that proved the vaccines I was given, and so deeply believed in, were effective. All I needed was one study to ease my scientific mind, just one piece of scientific research. And as I was trying to find this piece of evidence, I found myself moving further and further away from the deep-rooted beliefs I had held for so long—and closer to a very new reality.

Not only was I unable to prove to myself that vaccines were effective, I was in awe at how much harm these vaccinations have caused. There is a very moving quote from Dr. Tenpenny that I want to share:

> If a "dirty bomb" exposed a large segment of U.S. citizens simultaneously to hepatitis B, hepatitis A, tetanus, pertussis, diphtheria, haemophilus influenza B, three strains of polio viruses, 3 strains of influenza viruses, measles, mumps, and rubella viruses, the chickenpox virus, and 7 strains of Streptococcus bacteria, we would declare a national emergency. We would call it an "extreme act of BIOTERRORISM." The public outcry would be immense and our government would act accordingly. And yet, those are the very organisms that we inject through vaccines into our babies and small children, with immature, under developed immune systems. Many are

given all at the same time. But instead of bioterrorism,
we call it "protection." Reflect a moment on that irony.[11]

If you believe that vaccines are safe and effective, then you owe it to yourself to find the proof that supports your beliefs and your decision to vaccinate. Vaccinating your child is a decision that can possibly change your life and your family forever. For the sake of your child, your family, and yourself, make sure you make a decision based on your own knowledge. Then I suggest that you only work with healthcare professionals who support your decision and are willing to have a conversation with you about your choices.

What's in a Vaccine?

It is worth your time to look into the specific pharmaceutical concoctions known as vaccines. If you're considering vaccinating your child, there are a few major variables to take into consideration. To begin with, please look into your family's medical history and your child's risks. What is your child's medical disposition? The National Vaccine Information Center (www.NVIC.org) has created a list of eight questions (Ask8) to consider before you vaccinate. I believe it is crucial to consider the answers to these important questions, to speak with more than one trusted health care professional, and to educate yourself fully and thoroughly, so that you are confident in your opinion about vaccination. The science and all the answers to your questions are readily available. You simply have to begin your quest.

In the earlier part of this book, I mentioned Dr. Michael Gaeta, who is an acupuncturist, nutritionist, speaker, health activist, and the health practitioner who introduced me to a holistic lifestyle. He has studied and researched vaccines for many years, and now educates medical doctors across the nation about immunizations. His seminars fill the rooms and are very successful, since this controversial subject is now one that many doctors truly want to educate themselves about. Throughout this chapter, I

---

[11] www.newswithoutviews/Tenpenny/sherri1.htm

will be mentioning information he shares during his well-attended medical seminars on vaccines.

According to Dr. Gaeta's extensive scientific research, vaccines manufactured by pharmaceutical companies present serious health risks to children, and actually do not prevent disease. What is causing these serious health issues are the ingredients in vaccines, which include mercury, formaldehyde, aluminum, ammonium sulfate, and aborted fetal tissue, to name a few. These are all harmful to the immature immune system of the infant.

Earlier, I also mentioned our family's pediatrician, Dr. Lawrence Palevsky. He is also known throughout the country for his knowledge of vaccines. Dr. Palevsky is a highly-respected holistic pediatrician, and his opinion matters, which is why he is often interviewed by magazines and other media. On his website and in an interview with Dr. Joseph Mercola,[12] he says that at some point in his career it became clear to him that "vaccines had not been completely proven safe or even completely effective," and that "conclusions made about vaccine safety and efficacy just did not fit the scientific standards that I was trained to uphold in my medical school training." Palevsky says that more studies are coming out every day, which show, "There are particles in vaccines that *do* accumulate in your body and cause impairments in your immune system; there are particles in the vaccines that get into your brain, and there are foreign DNA particles that get into your body."

Dr. Palevsky says that in the ten years he has been investigating vaccines, he has seen the negative effects they have on children in his own practice. He states that according to his experience, he has seen, "Many of these kids who were developmentally normal, who were doing well, who were speaking, then whose voices and eye contacts were lost, who went into seizures, who developed asthma and allergies, and they [the parents] had nowhere to go because their doctors told them that they don't know what they're talking about."

He often saw a child regress immediately after a vaccination. He says the literature shows that vaccines are having an effect on the immune system of children, particularly if they are vaccinated before they are

---

12   Interview with Dr. Joseph Mercola, "Expert Pediatrician Exposes Vaccine Myths," November 14, 2009, http://articles..mercola.com.

one year old. As he has observed, "More and more of these kids who are suffering from chronic illness are suffering from impairments of their immune system." And literature today shows that vaccinations play a role in this impairment.

Unfortunately, these pharmaceutical cocktails have gained much attention and are now in the spotlight for causing a large number of ailments in the children of our world. One controversial ailment, which research has shown to be linked to vaccine injury, is the rise in the number of cases of autism, particularly in the U.S. This prevalence of autism was not the case even 20 years ago. Countries like Japan and China never had any reported cases of autism until they began to vaccinate. In country after country, where the vaccines are now being exported, we see that where autism never existed, it suddenly appears shortly after the introduction of vaccines. It doesn't take an expert to figure this one out—nor is a scientific study necessary, in my opinion.

Mercury, a substance which has been used as a preservative in vaccines, has definitely been linked to autism. Dr. Gaeta says, "According to epidemiologist Tom Verstraeten, who has analyzed the agency's [American Academy of Pediatrics] massive data base containing medical records of 100,000 children, a mercury-based preservative in the vaccine, Thimerosal, is responsible for a dramatic increase of autism and a host of other neurological disorders among children."

Thimerosal was labeled by the military as a poison, and is one of the most potent neurotoxins, destroying brain and nerve tissue. It was mandated that the pharmaceutical companies remove Thimerosal from vaccines in 2003, but doses already on the shelves and in warehouses can still be sold. And, believe it or not, the mercury-based preservative is still used in flu shots, according to the Center for Disease Control (CDC).[13] There is no definite answer as to whether Thimerosal is still present in other vaccines that are currently administered, or how much of it still shows up in today's vaccines.

---

[13] http://www.cdc.gov/flu/protect/vaccine/thimerosal.htm.

Do Vaccines Promote Health or Disease?

The sad part is that it does not stop at autism. Vaccines are linked to various forms of learning disabilities, neurological disorders, diabetes, asthma, and allergies. One serious health risk is mentioned by Dr. James Strain, past president of the American Academy of Pediatrics, who says, "Our main concern is with the Pertussis [whooping cough] vaccine. One in 3,000 doses causes permanent injury to a child." Dr. Gaeta comments, "Now do the math. Each child gets four of them... You have 1 in 750 children and babies, globally, who are being permanently injured by this vaccine." He adds that a study showed, "Significantly, a 26% rise in the incidence of diabetes occurred in children who received the Haemophilus (Hib) vaccine."

An alarming study done recently, which provides us with objective data about the negative effects of vaccines on newborns, is worth mentioning. During the study, newborn primates were given a single dose of hepatitis-B vaccine containing the mercury-based preservative Thimerosal. The vaccine was given within 24 hours of birth (in the same way our newborn children are vaccinated in the hospital). The control group received either a placebo or no vaccine. In the exposed primate infants, a significant delay was found in the development of basic reflexes, compared with no delay in the control group. Lower birth weight and gestational age exacerbated the adverse effects of vaccine exposure, showing that those infants were more vulnerable. The study concludes, "This primate model provides a possible means of assessing adverse neurodevelopmental outcomes from neonatal Th-containing hepatitis B vaccine exposure, particularly in infants of lower GA [gestational age] or BW [birth weight]."[14] Considering the results of this and other studies can help parents make informed choices.

There are many more studies like this one that are very clear about the adverse effects of vaccines, which you can read about yourselves on the NVIC website. Every second you spend researching the scientific evidence is well worth it.

---

[14] Hewitson L, Houser LA, Stott C, et al., "Delayed acquisition of neonatal reflexes in newborn primates receiving a thimerosal-containing hepatitis B vaccine: influence of gestational age and birth weight," *J Toxicol Environ Health A*. 2010;73(19):1298-313.

What Do the Vaccine Inserts Say?

If you simply read a vaccine insert, you will be surprised or even shocked to learn about the side effects mentioned by the manufacturers themselves. These are also due to other ingredients that vaccines contain, like aluminum. In 1996, the American Academy of Pediatrics issued a paper, "Aluminum Toxicity in Infants and Children," which stated in the first paragraph, "Aluminum is now being implicated as interfering with a variety of cellular and metabolic processes in the nervous system and in other tissues."[15]

In 1994, studies showed that one in six children under the age of eighteen in this country have developmental or learning disabilities. Is it possible that this metal is affecting and "interfering" with the metabolic process in our children's nervous systems and causing this constant rise in developmental and learning disabilities? I'd say this would be a good subject for a future scientific study, so that we can find out if there is any correlation. And if there is none, in addition to what the study mentions above, what else can a metal like aluminum do to our babies' bloodstreams when we inject it into their veins?

What about the ingredients of formaldehyde or polysorbate 80? What potential risks do these ingredients cause to our children's health and neurological development? I would like to see studies answering these questions. These answers are crucial. And so, since there are no such studies, we have to go by what the scientific community says these substances can cause in humans–which according to them is detrimental, and can even be fatal.

These are a just a few of the many questions that we should ask when it comes to such a hotly debated topic like whether to vaccinate or not. If the jury is still out, then, as parents, it is up to us to make an educated decision about what goes into our children's bodies.

Got the Flu?

Since we're on the topic of vaccines, I also want to talk briefly about flu vaccine (or flu shots). According to Michael Gaeta's seminars, the CDC

---

[15]   Committee on Nutrition, American Academy of Pediatrics, *Pediatrics* 97 (1996): 413-416.

has reported, "There is low effectiveness against influenza or influenza-like illness [from the flu shot]. Depending on how the data were analyzed, the vaccine protected from 0% to 14% of the study participants." So if it's hardly effective, why take it?

Certain flu shots contain live viruses, which can spread infection into the community. In fact, the vaccines with live viruses are not recommended for people with suppressed immunity. As for the shots with an inactive virus, Dr. Gaeta quotes a study showing that the trivalent inactive influenza vaccine had no or low effectiveness against influenza-like illness. The problem is that this concoction can cause Guillain-Barre syndrome, an auto-immune disease, and is associated with a 432% increase in the incidence of Guillian-Barre.

A connection has been shown between flu shots and Alzheimer's, too. According to Dr. Gaeta, "One of the most brilliant, widely-published genetic biologists ever, showed in his research that five consecutive annual flu shots increased the chances of developing Alzheimer's disease to 10 times greater than if they had zero, one, or two shots."

Through my research and numerous conversations with health professionals, and consulting books, articles, and DVDs, I've found that *nothing* out there proves that vaccines actually work—*there is not one scientific study to prove their efficacy*. I ask my readers to look into this themselves and educate themselves, instead of taking my word for it, or anyone else's. The most frequent comment I get about this from mainstream doctors is that vaccines have eradicated disease. Please take a better look at the statistics and the charts. These diseases were being eradicated prior to the introduction of the vaccines.

"...They say, that our children need to be safe, based on nothing, no science, no data, no evidence, and no proof," Dr. Gaeta tells doctors at his medical seminars. According to the data he has organized, the so-called success of vaccines in eliminating diseases was due not to the vaccines, but to the fact that these diseases were on their way out anyway, because of better nutrition, sanitation, and hygiene in society as a whole, and society's natural adaptation to pathogens. "The number one reducer of infectious disease globally is sanitation and hygiene," he says.

What About Polio?

When I am talking about vaccines, many people ask, "What about polio?" And my response is, "Yes, what about polio? If you believe that polio disappeared due to vaccinations, please provide the scientific research to back it up." First, let me say that polio will never disappear. This is because the scientific community proudly discovered its genome in 2002, recreated it, and now can always recreate it in vitro. Anyone with the right background can now make polio, and so it is not going to ever fully disappear. Secondly, the information I have read from statistical graphs shows that polio was already on its way out prior to the vaccine's introduction. In the following page, I have included a few graphs that clearly illustrate how disease and viruses declined prior to the introduction of vaccines. These graphs were created from information provided by government statistical health agencies in various countries. In the Resource section you will find more information that refer to additional graphs similar to these.

Graphs Showing Decline of Diseases
Before Introduction of Vaccines

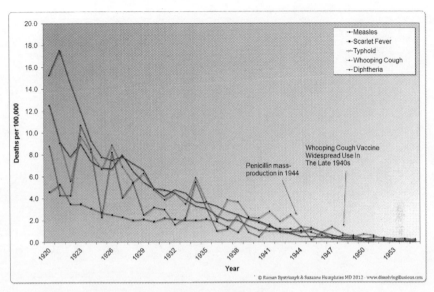

US Deaths 1920

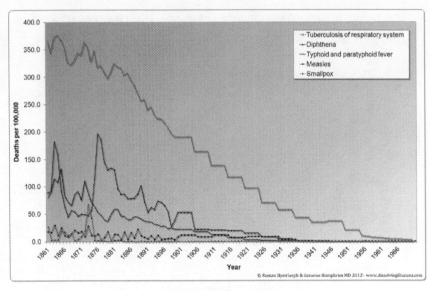

MA Deaths 1861

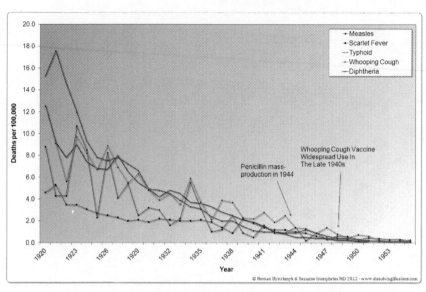

Pertussis Graph

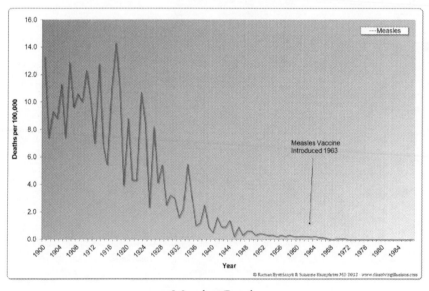

Measles Graph

If you are wondering how this could be so, the quick answer is that all viruses have a life cycle, and then they die off. For all the specific details about polio, flu, and any other inoculations, a good place to begin is with the DVD *Vaccines: The Risks, the Benefits, the Choices* by Dr. Sherri Tenpenny. She clarifies rather nicely what happened to polio and all the other viruses we vaccinate for. She has included the results of over 8,000 hours of research, and that should save you some time. Of course, you can research her conclusions, and make your own decisions.

I read something by Sayer Ji, founder of GreenMediInfo.com, who expands on the subject, shining a light on the polio myth:

> Due to the fact that polio spreads through the fecal-oral route (i.e. the virus is transmitted from the stool of an infected person to the mouth of another person through a contaminated object, e.g. utensil), focusing on hygiene, sanitation, and proper nutrition (to support innate immunity) is a logical way to prevent transmission in the first place, as well as reducing morbidity associated with an infection when it does occur.
>
> Instead, a large portion of the world's vaccines are given to the third world countries as "charity," when the underlying conditions of economic impoverishment, poor nutrition, chemical exposures, and socio-political unrest are never addressed. You simply can't vaccinate people out of these conditions, and as India's new epidemic of vaccine-induced polio cases clearly demonstrates, the "cure" may be far worse than the disease itself.[16]

When you begin looking into the past, you will notice that at the same time polio began to wane, the First World began installing more sewer systems and replacing cesspools and wells. After the war, city populations were on the rise, the housing boom began, and so there was a mass expansion of sewer installation to keep up with sewage elimination. Wood pipes and deformed pipes were constantly being replaced and the demand for fiber sewer pipes and PVC pipes skyrocketed. Rivers, where

---

[16] GreenMedInfo.com, January 17, 2012.

people used to swim (and where fecal matter could thrive) began to be cleaner. It became rare to see sign postings like "No swimming due to polio" at the Hudson River. As sanitation and hygiene improved, polio slowly became a memory.

Polio endemic areas are places where raw sewage flows into bodies of water. Polio still exists even after numerous vaccination campaigns in India and Africa where sanitation and hygiene have not improved, and people swim, drink, and eliminate (urine and fecal matter) all in the same river. Now these countries, unfortunately, are also dealing with the live polio vaccine virus strain, which has the same effects as polio, meaning that a child who was given the live oral vaccine and has an adverse reaction to the polio vaccine may become fully or partially paralyzed for life. In fact, during the last vaccine campaign in India, 47,500 children were paralyzed from polio.

So to sum up the polio myth, remember that the polio virus lives in the body's intestinal tract—it is spread through the oral and fecal route. In other words, good hygiene is the first way to stop the spreading of this virus, followed by sanitation and a clean supply of drinking water. If you want to explore the subject further, see the Resources section in the back of the book.

To better understand the polio vaccine, it is important to know that the inventor of the first polio vaccine, Jonas Salk, M.D., was pretty honest about its efficacy, but many people don't read his own statements about his invention. During his testimony in 1977, along with other scientists, he stated that mass inoculation against polio was the cause of most polio cases throughout the U.S. since 1961.[17] During the 1962 U.S. Congressional hearings, Dr. Bernard Greenberg, head of the Department of Biostatistics for the University of North Carolina School of Public Health, testified that not only did the cases of polio increase substantially after mandatory vaccinations, but there was a 50 percent increase from 1957 to 1958, and an 80 percent increase from 1958 to 1959.

I found the information and testimony about the polio vaccine really interesting, to say the least. Even more interesting is how research shows that in countries where the vaccine was not introduced at all during this

---

[17]   *Science,* April 4, 1977, Abstracts; Global Vaccine Awareness League, www.gval.com/facts.htm.

time, polio simply disappeared. So to answer the question, "Didn't polio disappear because of vaccines?" I would say that based on the science, the answer is no. In fact, the inventor of the vaccine testified that it increased the polio cases. And so when you do your research on vaccines, it would be a good idea to also look into the natural life cycle of viruses.

Why is There An Increase in Mandatory Vaccines?

Any thoughtful parent today has to at least wonder why their children are receiving so many more vaccines than we did as children. In fact, in 1983, there were 7 vaccines on the vaccination schedule, recommended for children from 6 months to 16 years old. Currently, our children are receiving 34 doses of 10 different vaccines. This does not include the flu shot or Gardasil, which are in the media every week due to resulting fatalities and various life-altering side effects. Again, when I was looking into all of this, I couldn't help but wonder why my child would need three times the number of vaccines that I had as a child. Is there any sort of epidemic or deterioration of quality of life taking place? And why are our children suffering from so many more debilitating ailments such as paralysis, neurological disorders, learning disabilities and much more? Something about this just did not make sense, especially since, as I said, most diseases can be treated and eradicated through simple methods such as hygiene and maintaining a strong immune system.

Currently, almost all the vaccines given are for non-fatal diseases, and according to Dr. Gaeta and sources from the alternative medicine community, dealing with mild infections can actually be beneficial to the immune system of the child. "The immune system, in short, is like a muscle. When you work a muscle, it gets stronger," Dr. Gaeta says.

If you believe that vaccines are safe and effective, then you owe it to yourself to find the proof that supports your beliefs and your decision to vaccinate. Vaccinating your child is a decision that can possibly change your life and your family forever. For the sake of your child, your family, and yourself, make sure you make a decision based on your own knowledge. Then I suggest that you only work with healthcare professionals who support your decision and are willing to have a conversation with you about your choices.

Compensation for Vaccine Injuries

If you have decided to vaccinate, and you or your child are injured after a vaccine is administered, one of the few things you can do is to seek minor compensation as a result of a very important act that was introduced in 1986. The NVIC (National Vaccine Information Center) worked with the U.S. Congress to pass the National Childhood Vaccine injury Act of 1986, which allows for the possibility of receiving compensation to assist with the medical costs that arise after an injury from vaccines. These medical costs are often crippling to a family and often lead the families of injured children to bankruptcy. Although two out of three applications have been turned down, this fund is the only place families can turn to for financial compensation. For an excellent discussion of this topic, see the NVIC website, at **www.nvic.org/injury-compensation.aspx.**

Vaccine Manufacturer Immunity

Vaccines are the one class of drugs that are exempt from the many requirements for safety and efficacy that the FDA imposes on pharmaceutical drugs manufactured and sold in the U.S. It is important to keep in mind that vaccines might be "recalled" for the same reasons that pharmaceutical drugs are "recalled." These stories are in the news often, and for these drugs to be recalled, it has to be proven that they cause death or other serious side effects. The difference is that vaccines are mandated by law, and they do not get recalled—ever. The very vaccines our country insists that we give our children to protect their heath are made by the same pharmaceutical companies that make drugs, which are recalled due to harmful side effects. And because vaccines are not regulated to the same standards, it is highly likely that they contain substances that will weaken our children's health and immune systems.

The problem here is that the manufacturers (of most vaccines) have been given complete protection by the government, and so if you suffer any side effects or injury, you are pretty much on your own. The side effects of vaccinations are very real and are mentioned in the manufacturer's own inserts or, as previously mentioned, on the CDC website. Under the Act of 1986, hundreds of millions of dollars in vaccine injury claims have been paid out to parents, but as part of the Patriot Act of 2011, according to Dr. Gaeta, almost all drug companies are now "shielded from any liability for any vaccine ever given." In fact, after my latest research on this, I learned that every few years, there are new acts and bills signed into law that exempt the pharmaceutical companies from paying for damages caused by their vaccines, including the newer ones, such as the swine flu vaccine.

After learning about all this, as a mother, the one request I have to the pharmaceutical industry, the FDA, and our government is to please conduct at least one *valid* study where vaccinated children versus unvaccinated children are tested and studied to see if there is any difference in health and immunity between the two populations. (I'm suggesting this be done some time after one group has received all the vaccines on the current schedule.) I strongly urge every mother, no matter where you stand on the topic, to make that very same request. This is a good step towards truly keeping our children healthy.

When to Legally Not Vaccinate

If it is your sincere religious, philosophic, or conscientious belief not to vaccinate, you will also need to learn what to do when the time comes for your child to attend school. Each state has its own laws when it comes to vaccine exemptions, and I urge you to browse the NVIC website in order to find out about your local laws, and what steps you need to take from there. In many states, parents can opt out of vaccinations by requesting an exemption on philosophical or religious grounds. Only Mississippi and West Virginia have laws forcing you to vaccinate. Doctors can't advise you to opt out, but you can find doctors who "don't mind" if you do, and who will work with you. I have added a few helpful websites in the Resources section for additional help.

Vaccination Choice

Many holistic health practitioners, such as Dr. Gaeta and Dr. Palevsky, do not advise parents not to vaccinate their children, but instead, provide them with information so they can make their own decisions. If parents finally do chose vaccination, holistic health practitioners advise them not to vaccinate a sick child or one with a weakened immune system, and to insist on single-dose vials, since the multi-dose vials have the most aluminum and mercury. Dr. Gaeta also suggests using positive imagery, visualizing that the vaccine will help your child, and not do harm.

The topic of vaccines has grown to be a very controversial and hotly debated one. Every year, the number of parents opting to either not vaccinate or to use an alternate schedule increases in our country. Parents are realizing how important it is to begin researching and inquiring about this subject. In addition to the information I have given in this chapter, remember to also check in to see how you feel about it. If feelings of fear and doubt arise, that is your clue to examine your decision. A life-altering decision such as this one should never be guided by fear. It should come from a place of truth within you. If fear is dominating, gain more knowledge to calm the fear, and reach out to others to hear how they overcame their fears. This may help you to hear your inner voice, and you can then begin to take your first steps towards what you feel is right.

I am hopeful that you will find all the support that you need to explore this important subject, so you can make a decision you can feel good about. It is imperative that we do this for our children.

CHAPTER 16

Garments And Accessories

Whether you are creating your first baby registry or deciding to recreate a whole new nontoxic environment for your child, it is now easier than ever to do so. There are now more options available, thanks to the great demand resulting from a movement of newly-educated and mindful parents. It is mind blowing to think about what children have been exposed to in the last 20 years. It is no surprise that there has been an increase in childhood illnesses. The reasons for these diseases are many and cannot be narrowed down to just one cause. However, I would like you to consider what effect the exposure to simultaneously combined toxins and off-gasses could have on our children. This is why we should be more careful, conscious, and informed when making any purchases for our healthy little babies.

We Can Do Better

The amount of toxins found in the items our children are exposed to is almost unbelievable, and, dare I say, even criminal. Ranging from petrochemicals, BPA, PVC, phthalates, heavy metals, gases, coal ash, flame retardant chemicals—you name it, and it is not possible for our children to safely absorb these toxins every second of their lives. We are, however, blessed to have the option to keep their exposure to a minimum.

And for whatever we cannot control, there are ways to eliminate these poisons from their bodies.

I want to share with you a great statement by John Breeding from a *Pathways to Family Wellness Magazine* article that I like to use as an affirmation. I find this to be a mindful, yet relaxed way to discuss the subject of product toxicity. Breeding writes in his manifesto:

> I recognize that as a parent, it is my responsibility to protect the well-being of my family from the dangerous and detrimental practices of our Western society. Therefore, I have vowed to keep my eyes open, to educate myself, and to provide protection for my children to the best of my ability against the most grievous harms.[18]

Thanks to this kind of thinking, we can now feel empowered instead of discouraged, depressed, or any other sort of unproductive emotion. Even conventional mega baby stores carry nontoxic, organic, clean products nowadays—so I believe that parents today have every opportunity to create a healthy, nontoxic environment for their children.

That said, when shopping for clothing, I encourage every parent to purchase organic cotton material whenever possible. Please look at the Resource section for a list of companies that provide items with clean, green, nontoxic material. Almost everything in my children's closets, ranging from undergarments, to clothing, raingear, snow boots, and winter apparel, is all nontoxic. Consider when your child is sweating and her pores are open, or when she is sleeping and her body is restoring and healing. Do you prefer that her body absorbs chemicals or harmless nontoxic material?

When purchasing teethers, pacifiers, bottles, or anything that will be put in your child's mouth, choose items that are labeled BPA, PVC- and/or phthalate-free. These chemicals are found in all plastic material unless labeled otherwise. If the label states that they don't contain these chemicals, find out what they are replaced with, because savvy manufacturers will simply replace BPA with another harmful plastic substance. These

---

[18]   "A 21ˢᵗ Century Manifesto for Parenting," *A Pathway to Family Wellness*, March 2010.

chemicals leach into everything they come in contact with, such as milk, hands, and so on.

When the chemicals enter a child's body, they begin to affect hormone levels, which studies have shown can affect their physical, mental, and emotional growth, and lead to infertility later on. There are many rodent studies showing that infertility is associated with BPA, but now we also have quite a few human studies that show that men with high BPA levels in their urine are likely to have very low sperm count and reduced sexual function.

I think it suffices to say that once we make it our goal to dress our children as healthily as we possibly we can, we find that there are plenty of places that provide a variety of whatever we are looking for. And of course, my cheat sheet and fast track options in the Resource section in the back of the book can make a mother's life much simpler. Have fun decorating and playing dress-up, knowing that your child is as safe from toxins as he or she can be. You will experience peace of mind with this kind of approach.

Chapter 17

Baby's Room

Hooray! You are ready to create the nursery or redo your child's room into a green, clean room. Congratulations! By now I think you realize that I am a firm believer in informed choice. Have you decided on your baby furniture yet? What color to paint the room? Or what the theme should be? My husband and I considered all these questions and spent a lot of time looking into colors and deciding on our theme and corresponding furniture at the baby store. Unfortunately, during my first time around, I wasn't really making an informed choice. By the time my daughter came around I had slapped myself silly a couple of times for not having looked into my son's room properly. As a researcher by nature, I was so embarrassed to have loaded his room with so many toxic items. But hey, you live and you learn. I am so grateful that all the other areas we were conscious in, balanced out the toxicity in his room (and body), and he is a rock solid healthy little man.

I can help by providing you with a cheat sheet for creating a healing sanctuary for your child. Needless to say, this applies for the entire house, since the little ones live in every room of the home.

Where to Begin

If you're starting with an empty canvas, what color do you see in your child's room—and what shade of that color? Will you have borders, chair rails? Whatever the answer, try and keep it "green." Your paint can be free of toxic chemicals such as volatile organic compounds (VOC's). Just so you know, if you see paints that state they have low VOCs or zero VOC's, they may still contain high quantities of toxic solvent chemicals that you simply do not want your perfect and pure infant to be breathing in during sleep. That is the time the body restores itself, and so it is crucial to make sure everything in their room supports restoration and well being. Most paints include poisonous chemicals such as formaldehyde, mercury, petrochemicals, and benzene.

Harmful Effects and Healthier Options

I will not go into all the studies that show the link between these toxins and cancer, neurological disorders, and respiratory diseases. You can always check that out yourself. Simply know that throughout their website and articles, the American Lung Association summarizes that VOCs can produce a number of physical problems such as: eye and skin irritation, lung and breathing problems, headaches, nausea, muscle weakness, and liver and kidney damage. VOCs are consistently ten times higher indoors than outdoors, with numbers rising to 1,000 times higher after a new coat of paint…something to be avoided if possible! For more information, you can visit http://www.lung.org/healthy-air/home/resources/carpets.html.

Your beautiful baby was in your sterile womb for nine months, where you made choices to ensure all was perfect and healthy. You can do the same once your angel comes home. There are many great eco paints that have absolutely no VOCs, are organic, eco friendly, odor free, look great on the wall, and even offer a large color selection to choose from. An example would be ECO's organic paints, which can be delivered right to your door. Please refer to the Resource section for more information on paints.

Once you have decided on the brand of paint, you can then have fun picking the colors. From my children's school, I began to learn about the importance of color when it comes to a child's environment. Many little ones are attracted to warm, bright colors. As they grow and mature, their environment changes, and so does their color interest. Hence the teenager who no longer likes pastel blue and goes for a natural green or red instead.

For an infant and young child, colors such as pastels, soft pinks, oranges, yellows, and blues offer a very cozy and inviting feeling. Too many colors and images can be straining for a young child, so keep the color simple when browsing the color chart.

Most of these eco paint companies also make and carry organic, nontoxic wood finish or stain. If you're planning on having a wood floor in your child's bedroom, opt for a nontoxic finish for the wood as well.

What's in Your Carpet?

If you're going to install a cozy carpet instead, again try and steer clear of the VOCs. Carpets contain toluene, benzene, formaldehyde, ethyl benzene, styrene, acetone, and a host of other chemicals, some of which have already made the EPA's list of extremely hazardous substances. Known carcinogens, such as p-Dichlorobenzene, are in most new carpets, and are chemicals that produce fetal abnormalities in test animals. These chemicals also cause hallucinations, nerve damage, and respiratory illness in humans. For more information, go to (www.epa.gov/oppfead1/safety/ healthcare/handbook/Chap16.pdf). You get the idea—and I'm not here to instill fear. I'm here to empower you. If you're really interested in learning more about the effects of paint and carpeting, see the Resources section in the back of the book for a few helpful ideas.

Now, if you can afford wool carpets, by all means please go for it, and you will thoroughly enjoy them. Since they are pricey, an alternative would be to purchase a carpet with as low a VOC rating as possible. Once installed, open all windows and allow the VOCs to leave your home. There is a bright side to VOCs, and that is that they evaporate within a few days, and then their emission is so low that you can no longer detect it. The atmosphere does get affected however, and if you're interested in preserving our planet and our children's future, it's not the best green option, but does offer less home toxicity. Your best bet may be to put down nontoxic wood floors with nontoxic finish, and then you can purchase a small organic area rug. Again, check the Resource section and my website, for a few places to shop for these products.

Window Dressing

So now that you've finalized the floor and walls, move onto the windows. Here you can be frugal and visit IKEA for inexpensive PVC-free blinds, or simple wooden ones. Nontoxic blinds are fairly easy to find. The same goes for organic curtains. I had my daughter's curtains ordered and custom-made online. I simply provided the measurements, and I picked the fabric. You can always make your own if you're able to, as well.

If you do sew, you may want to make your own blackout curtains, since there isn't much out there when it comes to a clean, green organic version. The cleanest version may be made by a company known as EarthShade, but, as of today, they are not 100 percent ideal. Blackout curtains are great for those night owls as well as your utility bills, but you don't want them off-gassing all day and night. And some of these can be pretty stinky. I remember running across some useful information about making your own blackouts by getting material from a site called **www.nikkidesigns.ca**. You may want to start there.

And now you have to decide on the furniture. If you have gone through the process of excluding VOCs in your child's room, you will probably want to make sure their mattress is VOC-free, too—and if possible, the crib as well. Your child will be sleeping directly on this mattress. I am so thankful that my daughter now has a brand new organic mattress, and believe it or not, it was donated to us by a fellow school friend. Why do you need an organic mattress? Well, remember VOCs? Yes, mattresses contain these toxic agents, such as polyurethane, and other toxic products. The chemicals in new polyurethane foam outgas into the air. It takes polyurethane between several weeks to several months to dissipate, depending on many variables. A mattress made with synthetic foams, batting, or fabrics must be treated with flame-retarding chemicals, so that it meets the federal open-flame flammability test. Whether a conventional mattress is made with standard polyurethane foam, memory foam, recycled polyurethane foam, Dacron, or even a combination of soy-based and polyurethane foams, there's no getting around the problem of flame retardants.

The flame-retardant chemicals in mattresses that contain any amount of polyurethane foam are called organophosphate chemicals. Unlike

VOC's, these chemicals do not become gases, are not easily detectable by smell, and levels may *increase* over time as the mattresses age. Even though the levels are low, since your child's body and face are on the mattress for a third of their lives (during their most sensitive restorative time), I suggest you purchase a chemical-free alternative.

As for the crib, most cribs are made of plywood or some sort of compressed wood that emits formaldehyde or a form of VOCs that leaks out from their adhesives. They are also usually treated with a conventional chemical stain. A simple and natural wooden crib is

> If you prefer to be eco-friendly about your wooden crib purchase, you can check out the Forest Stewardship Council for sustainably managed forests and see their suggestions of who to purchase furniture from.

your healthiest bet and will look just as beautiful as any other crib. It can be treated with a natural oil finish to preserve it.

You can check out the cheat sheet in the Resources section before you go on your first shopping spree.

What's the Verdict on EMFs?

When it comes to electromagnetic frequencies (EMFs), the scientific community is still very much divided on this important subject. When I see something like this being debated as it relates to health, I choose to simply take precaution until the verdict is out. Something is usually holding up that final say, and I'd rather not wait until it is all sorted out. So, in our home we have kept EMFs at a minimum to the best of our ability. We decided to keep most wires and electrical gadgets out of our children's rooms. My son doesn't have anything plugged in within his room, and my daughter at one point had her noise machine, which was placed as far away from her as possible. We kept the monitor away from her room and only plugged it into a nearby room if we really needed it. We could still hear her even if the monitor was in another room.

We also purchased a few EMF protection devices from EarthCalm that we have plugged into our home, and we also wear personal devices daily for a grounding effect. We keep our phones on "airplane mode" during sleep, and attempt to detox EMF radiation through our diet. Many of the greens found in the Green's First drink actually detox this form of radiation. There are also Young Living essential oils like Purification and Melrose that we apply for the same effect. I am including some research at the end of the book, in case you are interested in what the scientific community has to say about this, and which studies have found that EMFs are harmful and detrimental to our health. There is also a Call to Action for this important subject included. Radiation from EMF's comes from many sources such as our cell phones, cordless phones, laptops, PCs, televisions, and cell towers.

Keeping It Clean

At the end of the day, maintenance and cleaning of your child's room and your home are what work best in keeping pollutants out. It is possible, and it is not that expensive. Whether you open a window to air out the pollutants, clean with biodegradable nontoxic cleaners, or simply make sure there is no dust on the floor (or rug) or bacteria growing in the room. This is a very simple way to keep children's immunity strong as well as maintaining their overall health. If money is an issue, simple baking soda, mixed with lemon or vinegar, will clean your house spotless. If you add essential oils to that mix, then your homemade cleaner is unbeatable.

Our children's rooms and our home are a sanctuary. May you always remember to honor it, bless it, and take good care of it. In doing so, you are also taking care of yourself and your whole family. This is true wholistic living, where one component of your life seeps into and affects all of the others.

CHAPTER 18

Baby's Toys

This is a fun subject. There is so much to share on this topic, but I will try to keep this short and to the point. We all have witnessed a shift in the toy industry, as companies try and jump on the band wagon and add wooden toys back onto the shelves. That's great! They are hearing our voices and trying to make sure they stay in the game. However, please be wary of what you find at a conventional, mega toy store. Naturally, it all comes down to money for a mega corporate toy store. For us parents, it comes down to knowing the deal. And here it is.

There is a multi-billion dollar industry that markets to children, and children alone, and this marketing begins from the time our babies are still in our wombs.

We hear which belly music machine is better, which stories we can read to our bellies, which lollypops for prego's will help us with morning sickness—and this

> An excellent summary and jaw-dropping documentary on this subject is *Consuming Kids: The Commercialism of Childhood.* It reveals what is truly intended for our children by the marketing industry and how the current and future generations are impacted by it. It is a brilliant piece of work.

continues after the baby is born. Which gadget will get our baby to sleep longer, not spit up, which classical CD or DVD will get them to solve calculus problems by the time they are one year old, read by six months, speak foreign languages, and oh my goodness, this can drive anyone crazy.

The reality is that this does not stop as our children grow older, and before you know it, you have an entire house filled with toys that provide absolutely no value to your child. In fact, they are not truly educating or encouraging your child at all.

This is why Baby Einstein was sued and had to return the cost of all their DVDs to consumers — they are not educational. Nothing is—it is only to market and produce profits.

In fact, often times these toys are actually adversely affecting the natural development of your child.

A child does not need a battery-operated plastic, loud toy to teach him anything at all. It will not stimulate his natural, innate imagination. Your child is already born with a strong desire to learn, explore, and play. This is exactly what they should be doing. And if they are provided with some sticks, water, sand, and rocks, you will be pleasantly surprised to see your child's beautiful reaction, and what she can create with them. From about a year old, my daughter could play at the sink with gifts of nature or kitchen items for almost an hour. My son creates entire wooden block cities and villages, as well as puppet shows, from whatever he can find and put together. I enjoy observing him going deep into his own imaginative world. He is so absorbed sometimes that when I try to speak to him, it may take a few attempts before he can hear me. And this can go on for hours. This is all due to the lack of media, loud electronic toys, gadgets, and educational toys in his life.

The toys we have slowly converted to using are very simple, nontoxic wooden toys. They are BPA-free, Phthalate-free, PVC-free, battery-free, toxic-paint free. Most are simple wooden toys! Of course we do have a small number of plastic toys with some sentimental value because they were gifted to us and have meaning to my son. We have gently suggested to our friends and family that they don't buy as many toys for the kids, and if they do, that they purchase one small wooden item, if possible. For the rest of the well-meaning friends who do bring other items to our home, we donate them to Good Will at some point. We like to be in control of what our children are exposed to, because we can make a positive difference in their lives and our world. However, we are not here to change anyone.

Every few months, once holidays have passed, or after much has accumulated around the house again, we do a spring cleaning. We take a bag and go through the bedrooms, play room, and small living room toy basket and eliminate any broken toys, toys with missing pieces, plastic toys, and battery-operated toys, and then we give them away. We also go through the books and store more than half away, so that there is a smaller amount for our children to have to choose from when its night time. When all this is minimized, it feels to me like a breath of fresh air in the house—like I have more breathing room. It simply feels better, and what parent and child wouldn't want that?

Generally, the less the child has to choose from, the less overwhelmed and bombarded by options the child is. This makes their choices easier and less stressful. When there is an accumulation of stuff in the house, my son cannot tell you who bought what for him. However, when there is less stuff surrounding him, he values each object, and can tell you who bought the toy for him and for which occasion. He also cares for it more deeply. There was a time when my son would throw his toys around, break them, and be somewhat destructive. This was a hint to simplify by paring things down to a minimum.

I believe that the best mentor out there for simplifying is Kim John Payne, hands down. If you haven't read his book *Simplicity Parenting* for helpful tips on simplifying, I strongly recommend it. And while you're waiting for your book to arrive, you should check out his website, which provides many helpful tips as well. He explains how children here in the Western world are suffering from post-war syndrome, similar to what children in Vietnam experienced (only our children didn't experience war). Based on years of research, and from his own patients, he states that children are experiencing a different kind of war here, relating to consumerism and lack of simplicity, which results in our children being on more medications than any other children in the world. The main point here is to not buy into all the false information that mega corporations would like you to believe in. You and your family will appreciate the simple life. Slowly, invite simplicity into your life. Less is more!

CHAPTER 19

Loving Guidance

Originally, I was planning on calling this chapter "Loving Discipline," but personally, I have a difficult time with the word *discipline*. In our current culture, the agreed-upon form of discipline for any individual, no matter the age, gender, race, or ethnicity, is some form of punishment. I believe that this need for punishment often times misses the point. If we only punish, we do not correct from the heart, nor do we provide any opportunity to teach a better option. And isn't that what we want for our children? To teach them other acceptable options, which they can use to navigate life? I believe it is easy to see that there is a very flawed system in the U.S., which begins from the time our children are toddlers and continues to our overcrowded jails. Without an intention of teaching and guiding, we can expect that punishment alone will result in feelings of spite and resentment at one end of the spectrum, and anger and violence at the other.

Oftentimes, I have to reach deep within myself and observe my past, when it comes to guiding my children. As a child of two very different styles of parenting, I initially found myself very confused when it came to guiding my two-year-old son towards his true self and honest behavior. Like most people, my father and mother were my biggest teachers in life and parenting. My father never laid a hand on me, never raised his voice, and always talked me through everything. This goes as far back as I can remember, and I still enjoy the same relationship with him today. He has always been my best friend—someone I can trust and reach out to no matter what the situation. The love I have for him cannot be measured or described in words. When in doubt, I often ask myself what my father would do in my situation, and then the answers come to me. Often, I am in awe of the patience and love he had for his children.

My mother dealt with life and family very differently, and also gave me a tremendous amount to learn from. In the past, there were times when I would deny the memories of my mother sending me off with bruised thighs to play with my friends. Sometimes I would laugh at the recollection of her throwing kitchen objects at me. I drove her nuts. After school, I would run up the stairs to try and hide the wooden spoons and belts, so that she had nothing to beat me or my brother with. And even though she would threaten us about a beating prior to our getting home, I recall that I never really cared about what lay ahead of me—not until I opened the dreadful house door and reality hit—hard. This did not seem abnormal to me at the time, since it was common in our culture and I saw the same thing happening in many of my friend's homes.

The most challenging were my teenage years. I now realize that as hard as they were for me, they may have been even harder for her. I had grown to be extremely rebellious, and I admit that we hurt each other considerably and on a daily basis, until we moved to Europe. My father and brother didn't join us there for the first year, and my mother and I had no choice but to settle our differences. The truth is, that even though our relationship healed a lot at that time, we never really had a relationship or bond until I was in my early twenties.

Currently, I feel so fortunate to have a mother like mine. There are few people in this world with a soul like hers. She would give her life for her loved ones. Everything she ever did in her life was selfless, and it was all for her family, especially me. She barely knew how to handle the hardships which come with raising a family, and so she reacted in ways she later grew to regret. Honesty, love, and communication have helped us connect and support each other. Since the mending of our relationship began, it has been ongoing. I am grateful for this, because I know that I am able to lead a conscious, loving life as a result of our understanding each other better. This has led to a profound healing within me (and I hope her as well), which I could not have predicted.

My husband had a very similar experience with his two parents. And we have spent a lot of time trying to figure out how our parents' discipline styles affected us—and what kind of discipline we want to adopt for our own family. I share this because I want you to imagine my confusion when my son entered his first phase of "opposition." We wondered, how should we respond, now that he has begun to question us, test us, and act up?

Seriously, I was so lost. At the end of my long days, I would find myself emotional. I would ask myself, *where did my sweet little boy go*? He used to trust everything I said to him. He never disobeyed me, and although he had his moments, eventually he simply understood that mommy knew best, and he would trust my guidance. On the surface, this seemed to have disappeared, but in truth it never went away. My son was simply entering a necessary stage where he needed to explore and test everything—including his parents. This was his way of finding out what was right for him, and where he fit in his world. He was also sensing that his sister was on the way and wasn't sure what this change would to do his world.

With so much going on every day, I realized I needed a time when things were quiet in order to be able to tap in to my intuition. So, I often asked for guidance late at night, which was wonderful, because I would go to sleep knowing in my heart that my son was a sweet child, and this was just a phase for us to experience together. It was challenging on different levels, but the key was to try and stay clear, open, and loving—so that I wouldn't take any of it personally and react from that space. It's easy to get frustrated and feel vulnerable during these moments. That is when I turned to meditation. It helped me stay grounded, centered, and in control of my emotions and thoughts. The more I practiced, the easier it got, and I felt clear as to which direction and action to take during intense moments.

After I faced these challenges with my son, I discovered a very different side of myself. I experienced a healing, actually. I ultimately had to allow myself to feel that it was okay not to be my child's best friend. That is not the role I am supposed to play in his life anyway. Someone else will fit that part later on. Nor do I have to be a disciplinarian. I realized what I needed to do was to find a comfortable middle ground between the two that seemed right to me. I cannot say that this was a quick or easy task. And it will always be ongoing, as we face new challenges with each milestone.

How to Shift Gears

There are two remedies which I rely on after a difficult time to restore the closeness I have with my children. One is to simply go outdoors and reconnect with nature. There is no better way to ground, release, and pull yourself together again. If your children are going through a temporary or long-term period of just not being themselves, I encourage you to go to the beach, park, forest, or any place where your children can feel and play with sand, dirt, water, wood. Connecting to nature will spark and reunite all their senses with mother earth. (I did this often as a child and young adult and it worked miracles for me.) Do this for a few days, and both you and your child will feel a remarkable difference. It's pure therapy.

> If practical, go out and connect with nature almost every day. This will help balance out the sensory overload that children receive today by simply waking up to a new day. Oftentimes, children overreact and are out of sorts due to overstimulation, anyway.

We are found outdoors no matter what the weather conditions—we simply dress appropriately so that we can enjoy it. There have been times when our footprints were the first on the snow at our local park, and we knew we were the only ones there for days, since we would see no other footprints but our own during our next visits. We had the entire park to ourselves!

The second very useful remedy in our home was taken from Joseph Chilton Pearce's book, *The Biology of Transcendence.* I learned (from him) that I can stop myself in the middle of an escalating situation (or a sudden one). I take a deep breath, stop my thoughts, and put my hand on my heart, so I can focus on my heart and feel love flowing to the situation. This almost always helps me to ease up. It slowly reminds me that I can encourage a positive behavior as opposed to judging or reacting negatively to the incident.

When I practice this, I then move on to a suggestion that I learned from Kim John Payne. He suggests that when we talk to a child about misbehaving, we always refer to the action and never the child. It's the behavior that is not acceptable—not the child. Once the matter is addressed, it's also important to let the child know how loved he is, by giving either a hug or another loving action, thus communicating that it's love that is guiding mom and dad, not anger. Anger is not productive, nor will it lead to anything positive.

Of course, it's perfectly natural to feel anger. But don't forget, you model how you deal with emotions, and in all likelihood your child will copy what you do when he expresses his emotions. Wouldn't it be better if your child witnessed you dealing with an emotion such as anger in a healthy way? For example, instead of repressing it, you would allow it to express itself in a channeled manner. And I don't say this only for the sake of our children, but as a way of life. Sure, at first it may be difficult. But the more we do it, the easier it will get, as with anything else we practice often. The truth is that in order to be able to guide our children from our heart, we need to heal ourselves first. And in case you didn't have a chance to "clean house" prior to your parenting venture, your children will force you to take a deep, hard look at yourself and your past. You either mend and restore what needs attention in your life (past and present), or you allow it to affect you and your family until you choose to pay attention to what is holding you back. Children hold up that mirror whether you want to take a look or not. Should you choose to do nothing about your issues and hold-ups, you will ultimately have to deal with them again and again, as you witness your beloved child struggling through the same challenges you have. And if you were never able to work through it yourself, how will you ever be able to genuinely help your child through those times? This is definitely some food for thought.

Bumps on the Road and Reflection

If you are stuck and struggling through a very long, troubled phase with your children, ask yourself what could be going on. What is your child trying to communicate to you? What is going on within you or in your family dynamic that could be contributing to his difficulties? Tune in and see if there is something you haven't observed, either with your child or yourself, during this challenging time. As a new parent, I began to notice how my children responded to my emotions and different phases in my personal journey. With my daughter, I observed her go through an aggressive phase that lasted several months, with many ups and downs. I found that the reason why she was reacting this way to those around her was due to my own issues with aggression. Until then, I had not really embraced some pent-up anger, and dare I say, the "dark side" of me. I never knew how to channel anger or show anger in a healthy way. I shoved that side of me under the carpet for no one to see, and I never really had much guidance about it, until my daughter's behavior made me take a deep look within myself.

I did not want to disown my daughter's aggression, in the same way that I disowned my own aggression when I was her age. Apparently, I had to be clear within myself first about how I felt about aggression, before I could be clear with my daughter. After diving in and taking a better look at myself, along with doing personal work, I expanded to a very accepting place of who I am and how I manage my life emotionally. Once I began channeling the anger emotion in a healthy way, my daughter shifted her behavior immediately and was friendly and loving with everyone around her. Although she still experiences that emotion, she channels it in a much healthier way where it doesn't affect anyone. It was beautiful to witness her reaction to my work and growth.

And so I have noticed that every time that I am experiencing a transformation in my life, when I am addressing different matters, it affects my whole family. My children act out on what I am going through. And when all is resolved and growth has taken place, there is a feeling of peace within my family. And when love takes over, I witness my children being very affectionate with everyone around them. It is a pretty amazing reflection of where I am in life.

Just Be

I read a liberating piece of advice by John Breeding in the *Pathways to Family Wellness* magazine that said, "Children do not need perfect parents— just imperfect, good-enough parents who never give up!" Honestly, I read that after being a mom for about five years, and it shifted my perspective a lot. The truth is that most of us are faced with parent's guilt at one time or another, and conscientious parents frequently question whether what they just did could mess up their children for the rest of their lives. In the end, we are all resilient, and it's the love that will take us through each snake hole.

My viewpoint now is this: I know (and work on accepting) that no matter what I do, no matter how perfect I strive to be, I may have to apologize to my children for something later on anyway. I just have to be able to forgive myself for whatever it is, be woman enough to apologize, and simply be there for them.

Let go of perfection, and just do the best you can. Have faith in yourself, your child, and just keep it real—real to yourself and to them.

Moms—when I suggest you are "real to yourself," I mean also it is essential that you remember to be good to yourself. Yes, we are here for our children, but we need to be there for ourselves first. Otherwise, we won't have the inner strength to be the parent we really would like to be. I struggle with this myself when life becomes overly hectic; I find myself giving my all to my family, and by the end of the day there is nothing left for me. All the same, I feel the need to share that if you take the time for a yoga class, a manicure, or at least a five-minute meditation, you will feel so rejuvenated and eager to get back to your little ones again. And when it comes right down to it, you are also modeling to your children how to honor yourself, your time and your body. If you're teaching your children something while you're also honoring yourself, it's a win–win situation! So don't forget to enjoy your life at least a few moments a day.

And of course, don't forget to ask your partner, family, friend, or a sitter to jump in and help out with the load. Your partner would love to see you at ease and refreshed, and if they are able to contribute to that, chances are they would love to do it.

Once my children were no longer nursing, my husband and I began taking individual trips on our own or with our closest friends. Olga (my soul sister) and I went camping alone when I was pregnant with my daughter. I went to a few weekend bachelorette parties, and even to a Buddhist temple for a weekend retreat. I always came back a different person. And my husband was amazing with the kids, and the kids had a great time with him. My in-laws and friends have also watched the kids for a night out, and even an anniversary weekend. This time alone with a special person or your partner can truly do wonders, so remember to ask for it. The benefits trickle down to everyone!

There are many opinions, schools of thought, and methods of "disciplining" our children. Take from them whatever you resonate with, and follow your heart. You know how best to reach out and connect with your children. Don't judge yourself or them. It's all a part of learning and growth.

Meditation for Relaxation During a Heated Moment

Close your eyes and take in a long deep breath. Focus on just the breath. Place your hand on your heart. Do this again and again until you feel a change in emotion or a calmer feeling. You can do this in the shower, in the car, or on line at the market. Whenever you feel that your emotions are being fueled and about to take over, simply put your hand on your heart, take a deep breath, and go from there.

Meditation for Loving Guidance

Close your eyes, relax your arms, let yourself be heavy, and take in three long, intentional breaths—filling in your belly first and then your chest. Exhale from your chest first and then your belly. If thoughts arise, acknowledge them and let them go. Try to see your child not in his physical child form, but as a soul that has come here for a life experience. See him as you would see yourself, and let him know that you honor him and his journey here. Tell him that you are here to help him on his path in any way you can. Then see him as your child, your loving, good-natured child, and hold his hand to guide him. See him surrounded by his loving family and his angels. Send that image up to the sky and towards the universe. Slowly return to the present and open your eyes. Practice this at night before you go to bed.

Note: If you are confused and cannot hear your inner voice on any issue, ask for guidance right before you go to sleep. The answers will come in your dreams, through a friend, a book, or some other source.

CHAPTER 20

Media

"I fear the day when technology will surpass our human interaction. The world will have a generation of idiots."

"The true sign of intelligence is not Knowledge, but Imagination."

Albert Einstein

E instein was truly a visionary. I look around and I notice less interaction and socializing between humans, yet more time interacting on the phone or some other form of media. We have officially entered the "Information Age". A time when humans of any age (from infancy throughout adulthood) are engrossed in some sort of media screen - for almost the entire day. Holding a media screen in front of you for up to 7 hours a day has somehow become the new normal.

There was a time when everyone criticized Madonna and wondered why she did not allow her children to watch television. Here I am today, though, as a mother of a four-year-old who has never seen a TV program in her life, and a son who has hardly watched any television at all in his seven years. I have to admit, however, that initially, when he was six months old, I had him watching Baby Einstein videos in my car as I drove around peacefully from errand to errand. Little did I know that the company was later sued for false advertisement of educational DVDs. I figured it was only 15 minutes of viewing here and there, and it was harmless, because he never watched television at home. And to be totally honest, this was the best babysitter ever!

Deep, deep inside of me though there was a gnawing feeling that created a bit of doubt about even that small amount of exposure. It wasn't until he was 18 months old, when we attended our very first day of the parent-child program at the Waldorf School, that I learned about the negatives about children and TV watching. We were given an article to take home from the teacher, which scientifically explained all the detrimental side effects of television, and how they occurred within just a few minutes of viewing.

The information itself was shocking, but I did not expect to read that the American Academy of Pediatrics (AAP) also did not recommend children under the age of two years old watch any TV at all. Although it is tempting to sit your infant or toddler in front of the T.V., you may feel discouraged to do so after reading the vast number of memos and articles that the AAP has released, stating that parents should avoid this. The AAP refers to the crucial early years in a child's development and expresses concern out the impact media has on a child – especially for programming targeted to younger children, like all the so – called educational programs. In one of their articles they state:

"Pediatricians should urge parents to avoid television viewing for children under age of 2 years. Although certain television programs may be promoted to this age group, research on early brain development shows that babies and toddlers have a critical need for direct interactions with parents and other significant care givers (eg, child care providers) for healthy brain growth and the development of appropriate social, emotional, and cognitive skills. Therefore, exposing such young children to television programs should be discouraged".[19]

And children from two years old and up should only watch a limited one to two hours of any sort of media per day, in the company of a parent. I wonder if anyone was ever given this guidance from their pediatrician, or any other person for that matter? I would think that something this important would be written on the walls of our doctor's offices, and

---

[19] American Academy of Pediatrics, Media Education, Committee on Public Education. *Pediatrics* 104 Aug. 1999): 341-3. http://pediatrics.aappublications. org/content/104/2/341.long

available at schools, in program disclaimers, or any other place where children and their development are the subject of concern.

I quickly learned that the Waldorf School had a strict no-media policy, because it was their belief and experience that it affects the learning, social, and developmental ability of students—specifically their imaginative play. I began to read up on this subject, only to realize that this is yet another crucial subject that parents are not informed about, and not just misinformed, but also misled.

I was under the impression that media could help my child learn better, faster, and help them to be able to compete in their world. At least that is what all the marketing and labeling on the children's products led me to believe. I discovered only later that there are billion-dollar national media campaigns to convince parents of just this! If you are wondering whether there are any other billion-dollar industries, policy makers, or medical organizations that are currently compiling accurate scientific research in order to provide information about the dangers of young ones watching TV, the answer is no. Once again, it is up to the parents to do the legwork and then figure out what the healthiest policy is for their own family. Thanks to our computers, we can do just that with a click of a button (do it after your kids are asleep, though).

For those of us who think back to our childhoods and wonder about it, the answer is "yes," media has become more violent, graphic, sexual, and sadistic.[20] For almost a decade, the American Academy of Pediatrics has been citing studies on the negative effects of media, stating that in fact there are more than 2,200 studies that link various forms of media use with aggressive behavior. Media violence is especially damaging to children under eight, because they cannot easily tell the difference between real life and fantasy.[21] Research indicates that when they are exposed to media violence, kids can become more aggressive, insensitive to violence, have more nightmares, and develop a fear of being harmed[22]. A sample

---

[20]   "Violence in Media Entertainment," http://www.media-awareness.ca/english/ issues/ violence_entertainment.cfm

[21]   "Some Things You Should Know About Media Violence and Media Literacy," *http://www.aao.org/advocacy/childhealthmonth/media.htm*

[22]   *Pediatrics*, vol. 108, no. 5 November 1, 2001, pp. 1222 -1226, (doi: 10.1542/ peds.108.5.1222).

of 77 PG-13-rated films included 2,251 violent actions, with almost half resulting in death (UCLA, 2007). Witnessing that can be very scary for a child.

According to the Center on Media and Child Health at Children's Hospital Boston, American children aged eight to eighteen spend an average of 6 hours and 21 minutes daily using media—more time than they spend in school or with their parents. And the risks of spending this much time enthralled by what is on their screens are serious. I am grateful to all the updated research and science that clarifies how media viewing is now directly related to obesity, aggression, bullying, drug use, depression, vision deterioration, hearing deterioration, fear and sleep disturbances, anxiety, learning disabilities, radiation exposure, lack of imagination and creativity, and lack of motivation. I realize this is a long list, but I believe that as research continues, the list of detrimental effects will grow as well.

I remember reading about a 2003 study that found that toddlers and older children with screen media (which includes phones, computer, television, iPads, and any electronic device with a screen for viewing media) in their bedrooms learned to read later and read less than those with no screen media in their rooms. It is now also becoming clear that, not only are these "educational" shows not *truly* teaching our children anything, they are actually negatively affecting their learning abilities. I used to watch *Cookie Monster* and wonder if my child was picking up on his grammar. What if my child "learns" to speak like Elmo or Cookie? Well, he has watched them speak maybe a total of 15 times, and so he did not learn to speak from them—he learned from us. Yes, children learn to speak from their parents! They can learn almost anything from human interaction.

For example, they can learn to add by helping in the home when setting the table. To do so, they have to figure out how many forks, plates, and so forth, they need to complete the task. And they learn through all their senses, not just by viewing and hearing. This goes for simple as well as complex concepts, like understanding what happens in nature just by observing it while out on a walk. By speaking to our children, by playing and interacting with them, they will learn how to speak.

Believe me, I realize how tempting it is to turn on the TV when you need a shower or a few minutes of calm so you can finish cooking dinner. I admit that I employed the "TV babysitter" once my son was 13 months old, because it was the only way I could make my business calls. I will add this, however… the more I turned to the TV, the more I depended on it, the more my son asked for it, and the less he knew how to occupy himself, meaning that when I needed him to just play so that I could "do," he couldn't occupy himself for that long. Eventually I realized that the more he learned to explore imaginative play, the longer he would dive into his own world of play—and now he can play for hours on end. In fact, my son is actually busy playing somewhere in the house as I write this now.

What Do Children Engage in Without TV?

I also learned that if I didn't depend on TV, I could also become creative about how to engage my children in order to finish cooking dinner and other tasks. Instead of trying to keep them away or distract them, I include them. I know this can be challenging and frustrating at first, and you may be tempted to dismiss my advice, but try it a few times before you come to a final conclusion. Let them pour the salt, pepper, water, stir the food, or whatever they can do. For the most part they just want to watch. Sometimes they want to create their own mess or concoction in a bowl next to you. In time, your child will be prepping and cooking right next to you. My son now helps prepare our dinners. He also makes his own breakfast, sets the table with his sister, cleans up with her as well, and *absolutely loves* being a part of creating his meal. We always say that our food tastes so much better when we all cook it together, because of all the love spice that is put into it.

If you're looking for a way to occupy them when you bathe, just bring them into the tub with you to splash around and squirt water. Or have them bring their books and "read" on the bathroom floor as you shower. My daughter follows me to the bathroom and goes through my cabinet, taking out all items that look interesting to her. She washes up with me, listens to music, or looks through her books while I finish washing up.

My point is that you can get creative, and then you will realize that, not only can you live without the TV, you are better off without it. (Not to mention you will no longer hear nagging for the set to be turned on.) Slowly, your children will acquire the skill of being self-sufficient, since you do need your own time. Eventually, they will also understand what it means when you say "mommy time" or "quiet time." This also means they will come to understand "their time," which I can promise that they will cherish and value after a while.

What Lies Ahead

During the foundational years of children, if they are allowed to have all their senses nurtured, their creative process will blossom. This will pay off really well in their future. After the age of six or seven, if they express interest in media, they will be in a much better place to make their request—and to decide whether or not the program is fulfilling to them. As they get older, their decisions about what to view will come from a much better place. My children have come to understand that television is for older children or adults. They hear us watching it at night when they are in bed and never say anything about it. Sometimes they wonder why their same-age friends are watching it, and we simply say that this is what they do, and this is what we do— just like eating a different cuisine or going to a different school. The funny thing is that my son is up-to-date on most TV characters and can still play with friends who watch TV. He learns about all the shows through books, and so it is not like he is has no idea who Batman is. The book allows him the opportunity to create his own story afterwards too, and he has shared some really exciting ones with his friends.

If you're wondering how television is contributing to many of the major issues that parents and this nation as a whole are facing today, please read the articles and links mentioned in this section and in the Resources section. I strongly believe that if we do something about our children's television viewing, we will ultimately be improving our society and our world.

CHAPTER 21

Holistic Education

"The only thing that interferes with my learning is my education."

Albert Einstein

There comes a moment in the life of a parent when we wonder what will happen when someone else begins to teach our children about the world. Will that teacher be in sync with what we have tried so hard to teach our children? Will they contradict the values we hold dear in our family? Will they treat our child in the same loving, tender manner that we would? Will they care for this precious child when he needs it? All this comes up when it comes time to let go and trust that another adult will do just as well, or even offer more. Suffice it to say that the education our child receives must be in alignment with our family, community and lifestyle. I believe it is crucial that the home and school environment join forces, communicate, and collaborate so that the child receives similar messages in school and at home.

As wholistic parents, we made sure we found a wholistic educational system for our children, so that there would be a beautiful flow between home and school. We looked into several school systems and decided on the magical education of a Waldorf school. It is my strong opinion that this is one of the best educational systems there is, since it nurtures a child's mind, emotions, body, and spirit. It is through this nurturing that this kind of schooling is improving our world, one child at a time.

This explains why the Waldorf education is the fastest growing educational movement in the world today. There are currently 900 Waldorf Schools in 60 countries. More than 150 of them are in North America. There are also public Waldorf schools in Milwaukee and Michigan. There are 30 publicly-funded Waldorf schools, and many public schools throughout our nation are "Waldorf-inspired." I believe that as our global consciousness is changing, this education movement will be growing with it.

I will explain the philosophy behind it in a minute. But first I want to paint a picture through our personal experience, which resembles the experience of many Waldorf families.

I first took my son to the school's parent-child program, and upon entering the room, I knew that this was where we belonged. I felt many emotions, and I immediately took a deep breath. Our first experience was in a warm, welcoming, light pink-colored room, filled with soft drapes that were hanging throughout the ceiling, so as to provide a softer look above and around the room

There was a kitchen to my left similar to one that I would have had in my own home, with a sink, a drainer, an oven, a counter, plates, utensils, and all that would be needed in a kitchen. In front of the kitchen was a large, round wooden table and chairs, decorated on top with a candle and seasonal flowers, over a beautiful soft silk. The entire perimeter of the room was outlined with the most beautiful wooden toys I had ever seen, all prepared and ready to be played with. Wooden barns with animals, wooden horses, cars, trucks, a kitchenette with accessories and food, ironing board and iron, wooden strollers with cotton babies covered with blankets, wooden play stands, silks everywhere, and knitted animals all decorated this room. Honestly, walking into this room was like walking into a dream for me. My son dove right into this dream world and felt right at home. He hasn't left since.

As days passed, and we enjoyed our snack time discussions, I realized that this parent-child class was more like a support group for like-minded families. Our snack conversations became a sacred space where we shared our darkest and brightest moments as parents, and then we were lovingly guided by the teacher. We were slowly given the empowering tools and support to be the parents we wanted to be in our fast-paced world. We were learning how to calmly say "no" to the overwhelming pressures and fears that exist today for families, and listen to and trust our intuition more. At the end of the day, we were finding our voices and turning up the volume on them. As our mentors helped us increase our confidence, the external chatter was being drowned out.

This system of education is based on Rudolf Steiner's philosophy of anthroposophy. Without going into too much detail, I will say that this philosophy helped to create the modern day holistic lifestyle. It allowed the possibility of returning to our roots, and enjoying organic food, natural medicine, biodynamic organic farming, natural healthcare products, and a holistic education.

For the purposes of this chapter, it is important to note that the Steiner education nurtures the mind, body and spirit of a child. Steiner created a curriculum responsive to the developmental phases of childhood and the nurturing of children's imaginations. He believed that schools should cater to the needs of children rather than the demands of the government or economic forces. This is why he developed schools that encourage creativity and free-thinking, where each individual is guided towards their true essence and purpose in our world and to serve humanity.

This is the overall goal throughout the grades, starting from nursery school. The preschooler has the sense that the world is a good, interesting, and wonderful place. Toddlers are able to explore their surroundings without any inhibition. A child is encouraged to play, and through this method of learning, is then able to understand all the elements of nature, environment, and the world on a deeper level.

Each individual child who receives this type of education has the wonderful potential and ability to create a better world, and grow into an independent leader who can lovingly guide a group instead of following the mainstream. Children learn to guide from the heart, as their Waldorf experience allows them the opportunity to explore themselves, their world, and their universe with complete love and confidence. Steiner believes that only by allowing individuals this freedom, can they then fulfill their purpose on their journey in this world.

Fortunately, we have many options of education to choose from. Even public schools incorporate many different philosophies, and one can be more progressive than other neighboring schools. If you take the time to look around, do interviews, and research different schools, I am sure that you will find what suits you and your family best. And it doesn't have to be a black and white decision, either. What works for you for the first few years may not be such a good match later on, so go with the flow, depending on your needs at the time and how you and your family grows. In the same way that most parents and young adults research which college is the best match for them, you can use that same energy to research your child's first kindergarten class. This way you build a good foundation from the beginning.

Whichever school you research and decide upon, I hope it is aligned with all that you believe, value, and practice in your life. You may be delightfully surprised to find that there are options out there to nurture your child in ways similar to what you teach them as a parent. Go ahead and embark on discovering which educational philosophy is the best match for your family. What a blessed choice to have in your lives!

I believe that if we have a loving, wholistic environment at home, and we add a similar even more spiritual environment through our children's education, we are completing the wholistic world our children grow up in. If more and more of the younger generation are enriched with such an education, along with our guidance, I believe that more people in our world will be able to experience their lives in a wholistic and peaceful way. And why not? Wouldn't this form of education complement our home environment and clear the path for our children's, our Earth's and our humanity's future? I believe so. And I believe it's one of the most important investments you can make in your child's health and happiness, because it will serve him for a lifetime.

Conclusion

As I finish writing this message to parents, I want to say how grateful I am to be able to share my experience, and how much I hope that it helps others. Dr. B.J. Palmer, founder of chiropractic, once said, "You never know how far-reaching something you think, say, or do today will affect the lives of millions tomorrow." More than touching the lives of families, however, my goal is to help remind parents to listen to their inner voices in a way they never have before. I feel that the world is rapidly changing. We have chosen to have our children and bring them into this world now, and we owe it to them to guide them as best we can. The world needs as many strong, healthy, creative, loving, caring leaders as it can have to guide us in the future. I believe that in order for us to be the parents we dreamed of being, we need to first become attuned with ourselves, heal ourselves, heal our past, and continue to envision the future we always wanted. This, ultimately, will strengthen who we are as individuals and help us truly become loving role models for our children.

There is no one expert out there with all the answers. I assure you of this! There is no "one-size-fits-all" piece of advice, or one path for all of our children to take. We are all unique and different as parents, as are our beautiful children, and we are also all very much alike. So take from this book what you like and what resonates with you. Then feel free to tweak what you learned and customize it according to your own and your family's needs. And remember, your children chose you to guide them on their journey this time around. You envisioned the parent you always wanted to be before your children arrived. And so, keeping those two pieces of information in the front of your mind, may you embark on a life-long journey together, hand in hand, with open hearts, clear minds, and as loving souls.

With all my love,
Maria

Glossary

Some holistic Modalities and How They Can help

Acupuncture –This ancient practice originated in China thousands of years ago, and uses very fine needles to stimulate specific meridians or pathways, balancing the body's chi, or energy. Good for specific ailments, detoxing, and relaxation. Chinese medicine treats the body and mind as one.

Attachment Parenting – According to pediatrician Dr. William Sears, who coined the term, AP is based on responding to a child with sensitivity, nurturing touch, consistent loving care, and emotional availability, which makes for a strong parental bond and a secure child. Dr. Sears recommends baby wearing and bedding close to the baby. AP is responsive parenting, rather than a rigid set of rules, building trust between parent and child. (See **www.askdrsears.com** and website of Attachment Parenting International.)

Craniosacral therapy – Growing out of osteopathic medicine, this wholistic healing practice uses light pressure and touch on the scull, spine, pelvis to balance the central nervous system and promote healing.

Essential oils – The distilled lifeblood of plants, essential oils are highly concentrated, and large quantities of plants are used to create small amount of oil. Essential oils have been treasured since ancient times, and have many therapeutic benefits, from clearing infections to relaxation.

Holistic Psychotherapy – A body/mind approach to therapy, healing the blocks that stand in the way of our full potential, using Eastern and Western perspectives.

Homeopathy – Developed in the 1800s, homeopathy is a non-toxic and gentle form of healing that uses highly-diluted natural substances, according to the principle of "like cures like." Classical homeopathy treats the whole person rather than isolated symptoms, addressing the constitutional makeup of each individual.

Reiki – A form of hands-on energy healing, or "God-directed universal life-force energy," which originated in Japan in the early 1900s. Reiki enhances the body's innate ability to heal, leaving you more balanced, grounded, and open to your inner wisdom. Excellent to experience during pregnancy and after childbirth for mother and child.

Shamanic Osteopathy – A blending of osteopathy—which realigns the body's musculoskeletal system—and shamanic work, which helps explore the spiritual realms for healing. According to shamanic osteopath Dr. Nyree Abdool, the practice is a "multidimensional approach [to] understanding how thought patterns create one's emotional state and consequently [can] lead to ailments in the body."

Cheat Sheet
(a.k.a. Resource Pages)

RECOMMENDED READING

Coulter, Harris L. and Barbara Loe Fisher, *A Shot in the Dark: Why the P in the DPT Vaccination May Be Hazardous to Your Child's Health*, New York: Penguin, 1991.

Emoto, Masaru, *The Hidden Messages in Water*, Hillsboro, OR: Beyond Words Publishing, 2004.

Fallon, Sally, *Nourishing Traditions: The Cookbook that Challenges Politically Correct Nutrition and the Diet Dictocrats*, Washington, D.C.: New Trends Publishing, Inc., 1999, 2001.

Gawain, Shakti, *Living in the Light*, Novato, CA: New World Library, 1986, 2011.

Habakus, Louis Kuo, M.A and Mary Holland, J.D., eds, *The Vaccine Epidemic: How Corporate Greed, Biased Science, and Coercive Government Threaten Our Human Rights, Our Health, and Our Children*, New York: Center for Personal Rights, Inc., 2011.

Hay, Louise: *You Can Heal Your Life*, Carlsbad, CA: Hay House, 1985.

Kitzinger, Sheila: *The Year After Childbirth: Enjoying Your Body, Your Relationships, and Yourself in Your Baby's First Year*, New York: Charles Scribner's Sons, 1994.

Pantley, Elizabeth, *The No Cry Sleep Solution: Gentle Ways to Help Your Baby Sleep Through the Night*, New York: Better Beginnings, Inc., 2002

Payne, Kim John, *Simplicity Parenting: Using the Extraordinary Power of Less to Raise Calmer, Happier, and More Secure Kids*, New York: Ballantine Books, 2009.

Pearce, Joseph Chilton, *The Biology of Transcendence, A Blueprint of the Human Spirit*, Boston: Park Street Press, 2002.

Sears, William, MD, and Robert Sears, MD, et al., *The Baby Sleep Book: The Complete Guide to a Good Night's Rest for the Whole Family*, New York: Little Brown and Company, 2005.

Sears, William, MD and Martha Sears, RN, *The Breastfeeding Book, Everything You Need to Know About Nursing Your Child from Birth Through Weaning*, New York: Little Brown and Company, 2000.

Sears, William, MD and Martha Sears, RN, *The Discipline Book, How to Have a Better-Behaved Child from Birth to Age Ten*, New York: Little, Brown and Company, 1995.

Sears, William, MD and Martha Sears, RN, *The Attachment Parenting Book: A Commonsense Guide to Understanding and Nurturing Your Baby*, New York: Little, Brown and Company, 2001.

Singer, Michael A., *The Untethered Soul: The Journey Beyond Yourself*, Oakland, CA: New Harbinger Publications, 2007.

Tolle, Eckhart, *The Power of Now*, Novato, CA: New World Library, 1999.

GUIDE TO QUALITY SUPPLEMENTS

Standard Process – High-quality vitamins and supplements made from whole, organic foods grown on the company's own farms. Available primarily from health practitioners; some formulas can be ordered online.

<u>Rainbow Light</u> – Prenatal Multivitamin - Once-daily multivitamin and minerals in a base of superfood extracts, promotes baby's healthy development and supports mother's nutrition and energy.

<u>New Chapter</u> – Organic vitamins and herbal formulas, made mostly from whole foods, cultured in probiotics.

<u>Megafood vitamins</u> – www.megafood-vitamins.com
Closest in quality to Standard Process, made from 100 percent raw organic whole foods. Available in health food stores. Some formulas:

> Baby and prenatal vitamins
> Women's vitamin
> Kids One Daily with superfoods, vitamins, and minerals.

<u>Quality Greens</u> –

> *Greens First* – available through health providers and on Amazon. Helps alkalize body's PH; contains powered, whole organic greens, vegetables, probiotics, and other superfoods in tasty form.

> *Perfect Food* from Garden of Life– made from organic, raw juices, greens and superfoods.

> *Green Vibrance* – Includes organic freeze-dried spirulina, alfalfa grass, barley grass, antioxidants, immune support supplements, probiotics, and tonics.

Detox Supplements:

> *Renew Life Organic Total Body Cleanse* – 14-day cleanse, which includes herbal cleanse, fiber blend, and colon cleanse.

> *<u>Standard Process purification program</u>*. Includes six products for cleansing and detox.

Young Living – Essential oils are the liquid life blood of the plant. Using a few drops at a time of these high-quality organic essential oils can help clear up health issues naturally. They also offer supplements and body care products with oils. Available in health food stores, through a distributor, or at website www.youngliving.com. Some popular blends:

> Gentle Baby – helps relax and calm emotions –
> Thieves – supports immune system and prevents infection.
> Peace and Calming – use to diffuse in the room of infant or toddler
> Immupower – very effective for strengthening the immune system
> Young Living Detoxzyme – digestive enzymes for cleansing

Bach Flower Remedies – 38 flower remedies that work on a subtle level to correct emotional imbalances. Rescue Remedy is the most popular, good to have on hand for treating shock and emergencies.

Boiron Homeopathic Remedies – Source for wide range of homeopathic remedies, including arnica for injuries and Oscillococcinum for symptoms of flu.

ONLINE RESOURCES FOR NATURAL HEALING

www.westonpricefoundation.com – Website of Weston Price Foundation, based on the work of Dr. Weston A. Price, advocating nutrient-rich whole foods diet.

www.drmercola.com - Health tips from holistic doctor Joseph Mercola.

www.drpalevsky.com – Integrative pediatrician Dr. Lawrence Palevsky has a special interest in the health effects of vaccines. He's medical advisor to Holistic Moms Network, NVIC, and other groups.

www.gaetacommunications.com – Widely-respected author and speaker Dr. Michael Gaeta practices clinical nutrition, acupuncture, and herbal therapy; his website has links to articles and seminars.

INFORMATION ON BIRTHING AND PARENTING

www.lovecenteredparenting.com – Maria Gavriel's blog community on wholistic parenting, filled with loads of information, support and tips for the wholistic parent.

www.inamaygaskin.com – Ina May Gaskin, pioneer of the modern movement of midwifery, supports women's confidence in their natural ability to give birth, and the non-medicalization of childbirth; website includes links to useful articles and books.

www.simplicity parenting.com – A movement to simplify family life in order to raise calmer, happier, more secure kids; website offers a blog, trainings and workshops.

DVD: *The Business of Being Born* – 2008 documentary by Ricki Lake educates women about their birthing choices, empowering them to have the kind of birth they want to experience.

MEDIA AND EFFECTS OF TV ON CHILDREN

Johnson, Susan R., MD, FAAP, *Strangers in Our Homes: TV and Our Children's Minds, 1999, 2007 (revised) (article)*, www.thelizlibrary.org/liz/johnson/html.

Buzzell, Keith, *The Children of Cyclops: The Influence of Television Viewing on the Developing Brain*. California: The Association of Waldorf Schools in North America (AWSNA), 1999.

VACCINES – RESEARCH AND INFORMATION

Websites:

www.nvic.com – National Vaccine Information Center has a wealth of information about vaccines, including symptoms, reactions, and compensation for injuries. Their mission: "NVIC is dedicated to the prevention of vaccine injuries and deaths through public education and to defending the informed consent ethic."

www.generation rescue.com – Website for parents by parents about the connection between autism and vaccination, offering resources for diet and other support.

www.vaccinerights.com – Help with legal aspects, vaccine exemptions and waivers.

www.vaclib.org – Basic scientific and legal information about harmful effects of vaccines.

www.mykidsmychoice.com – helps parents legally and effectively refuse vaccines and help change exemption laws in the U.S.

www.drtenpenny.com – extensive resources from Dr. Sherry Tenpenny about health effects of vaccines.

www.vaccinesafety.edu – The Institute for Vaccine Safety of Johns Hopkins School of Public Health offers independent assessment of vaccines and vaccine safety

DVDs:

The Greater Good – award-winning film about the effects of vaccines on three families.

Vaccines: The Risks, the Benefits, the Choices, by Dr. Sherri Tenpenny –
information-packed film about the risks of vaccines.

Vaccine Nation by Gary Null – Film by nutrition expert challenges claims
of pharmaceutical firms and government health agencies about benefits
and safety of vaccines.

The Business of Being Born – 2008 documentary by Ricki Lake educates
women about their birthing choices, empowering them to have the kind
of birth they want to experience.

Graphs Showing Decline of Diseases
Prior to Introduction of Vaccines:

"Immunization Graphs: Natural Infectious Disease Declines; Immunization
Effectiveness; and Immunization Dangers," First Nations Centre,
National Aboriginal Health Organization, 2009. http://genesgreenbook.
com/ resources/ Natural_Infectious_Disease_Declines_Immunization_
Effectiveness.pdf

Health Sentinel – United States Disease Death Rates - http://www.
healthsentinel.com/joomla/index.php?option=com_content&view=arti
cle&id=2654:united-states-disease-death-rates&catid=55:united-states-
deaths-from-diseases&Itemid=55

INFORMATION ABOUT CHEMICAL
TOXICITY AND EFFECTS ON HEALTH

www.ncbi.nlm.nih.gov/pubmed – The National Center for Biotechnology
Information has info about the science of genomes and the link between
cancer and pesticides.

www.cancer.gov (website of National Cancer Institute) has links to studies
about the connection between pesticides and cancer.

http://www.epa.gov/pesticides/food/ risks.htm – information from the Environmental Protection Agency about the link between pesticides and cancer.

http://www.foodsafetynews.com/2009/12/study-finds-bpa-in-newborn-umbilical-cords/ - EWG research study on BPA leaking into fetus through the umbilical cord.

http://www.nytimes.com/2012/07/18/science/fda-bans-bpa-from-baby-bottles-and-sippy-cups.html?_r=0 –Article: "F.D.A. Makes It Official: BPA Can't Be Used in Baby Bottles and Cups," New York Times, July 17, 2012.

www.fluoridealert.org – Fluoride Action Network seeks to inform public about the toxicity of fluoride compounds.

EMF RADIATION

www.emf.mercola.com and www.earthcalm.com – Information on health effects of electro-magnetic fields (EMFs) from electronic devices.

www.drbuttar.com – Dr. Rashid A. Buttar's Center for Advanced Medicine and Clinical Research lists detailed facts about health effects of EMFs, and a call for action with ways to reduce EMF exposure.

ECO-FRIENDLY, GREEN, AND NON-TOXIC HOME PRODUCTS

www.ewg.org – Environmental Working Group – consumer's guides and research about environmental health research and advocacy.

www.epa.gov/iaq/voc.html – Information from the EPA about harmful VOCs in paint.

www.fsc.org - Forest Stewardship Council – Information about wood products from sustainably managed forests.

EDUCATION

News from the Waldorf education movement at http://waldorftoday.com

SPIRITUALITY

www.sharedheartfoundation.com – Counseling and workshops with spiritual orientation for couples and individuals by husband and wife team.

www.ramdass.org – resource for the work of honored spiritual teacher Ram Das and the Love Serve Remember Foundation.

www.krishnadas.com – traditional Indian chants and spirituality by the popular master of chanting, Krishna Das.

www.ions.org – Institute of Noetic Sciences - founded by Apollo 14 astronaut Edgar Mitchell, this nonprofit research, education, and membership organization supports individual and collective transformation and the development of human potential.

www.hellingerpa.com – Hellinger Foundation – home of Family Constellations therapy – Healing modality developed by Bert Hellinger to aid in healing the spiritual, genetic and emotional code carried down through the generations of a family.

ORGANIC CLOTHING

www.gardenkidsclothing.com – Small family-owned company, offering high-quality, 100 percent organic clothing, handmade in the U.S., with no flame retardants.

www.greenpeople.org – Guide to many companies that sell organic kids' clothing online.

www.kellyscloset.com – organic cloth diapers.

www.hannaanderson.com – wide assortment of organic children's clothing.

www.puddlegear.com – four-season raingear.

SOURCES FOR NON-TOXIC AND ORGANIC MERINO WOOL CLOTHING

www.novanaturals.com – wool, cotton, silk clothing, also toys and games.

www.nordicwoolens.com – organic wool, cotton and silk clothing.

www.greenmountainorganics.com – woolen clothing, organic bedding.

ORGANIC CRIB MATTRESSES AND BEDDING

www.theultimategreenstore.com – 100 percent organic mattress protectors, pillows, pillow protectors, sheets, blankets and duvets.

www.absolutelyorganicbaby.com – wide selection of high-quality organic crib mattresses, flannel receiving blankets, comforters made of wool, with cotton covers, crib sheets.

www.naturepedic.com – resource for organic mattresses.

BABY SLINGS AND CARRIERS

www.mayawrap.com – Maya sling – 100 percent cotton hand-loomed fabric, some styles available in organic cotton.

www.mykarmababy.com – Karma carriers – offers organic selections in hemp and cotton.

www.attachedtobaby.com – selection of cotton baby slings.

www.ergobaby.com – padded baby carriers.

CO-SLEEPERS

www.armsreach.com – Arm's Reach Co-sleeper. Carries many styles of co-sleepers, bassinets, organic bedding and mattresses. Also offers "the cocoon," swinging hammock sleeper.

TOYS

www.novanatural.com – natural toys, and games.

www.oompa.com – resources for healthy toys from companies around the world.

www.thewoodenwagon.com – natural toys from Europe.

www.magiccabin.com – distinctive toys, games, dolls.

CHILDREN'S FURNITURE

www.pristineplanet.com – Pristine Planet – furniture made of 100 percent chemical-free untreated wood, handmade, and non-toxic.

www.roomdoctor.com – Room Doctor Furniture Company – real wood, chemical-free furnishings, including platform beds, tables and chairs, book shelves, dressers and chests.

www.davincibaby.com – DaVinci Baby – environmentally-friendly cribs.

GREEN HOME RESOURCES

www.greenguide.com – green building resource guide.

www.the daily green.com – guide to green living at home.

www.greenandsave.com – information on energy saving, remodeling, with environmentally sound awareness.

www.ecosafetyproducts.com – manufacturer of high-performance green products for home building, including stains, sealers, and finishing.

www.fsc.org – information on Forest Stewardship Council.

NON-TOXIC WOOD FLOORING AND CARPETS

www.naturalhomerugs.com – natural fiber rugs.

www.greenamerica.org – flooring, directory of certified green businesses.

www.organicandhealthy.com – natural carpets and rugs, cribs and mattresses.

www.greenbuilding supply.com, na.pergo.com, and www.naturescarpet.com – web sites for non-toxic wood flooring.

www.thecarpetline.com – non-toxic flooring and carpets.

NON-TOXIC PAINT WITH LOW, OR NO VOCS
(VOLATILE ORGANIC COMPOUNDS)

Eartheasy – a guide to non-toxic paints at.

Ecos Organic Paints – www.ecospaints.com - high quality zero-VOC paint.

Green Planet Paints (mineral pigments) – www.greenplanetpaints.com.

Mythic Paint – www.mythicpaint.com.

Benjamin Moore paints offers the Natura label (they claim zero VOCs).

NON-TOXIC CLEANING SUPPLIES
FOR THE HOME

Gaiam – natural and non-toxic cleaning supplies – order online at www.gaiam.com.

Also organic sheets and clothing.

Ecover – Cleaning products for laundry, dishes, home cleaning, made from plant-based ingredients, sustainable, biodegradable.

Seventh Generation – green cleaning products, baby diapers, laundry detergent, paper towels, dish soap, tissues, paper towels, and baby wipes.

Low-cost organic cleansers can also be made at home. There are many websites offering ideas and recipes. A good resource is: Green Living Ideas, http://greenlivingideas.com/ 2008/04/27/natural-cleaning-recipes.

NETWORKS FOR HOLISTIC MOMS, ONLINE AND IN PERSON

Holistic Moms Network – www.holisticmoms.org

A non-profit organization connecting moms interested in holistic health and green living. "We encourage moms to trust their instincts, parent from the heart, use their innate sense of what is best for their children, live in balance with the Earth, and learn about the pros and cons of all healthcare and parenting options." More than 100 local chapters hold face-to-face meetings; there is also an online group, where active members can exchange information, and a monthly newsletter.

Waldorf Education – For parents interested in Waldorf schooling, there are online and in-person groups, and also Waldorf parents meet-up groups.

MAGAZINES:

Pathways to Family Wellness – quarterly print and digital magazine about conscious parenting published by the International Chiropractic Pediatric Association and Holistic Pediatric Alliance (HPA). Some articles are available free online at. www.pathwaystofamilywellness.org.

Mothering – At one time a print magazine; it is now published online at www.mothering.com, with a wide selection of articles and other resources searchable by subject.

MOTHER AND BABY YOGA

Yoga asanas for mothers to recover their strength post-partum, and for babies, to develop motor coordination. Offered at Baby Om in Manhattan and Brooklyn, New York, it's also a growing movement. www.babyom.com

About the Author

Maria Gavriel is a holistic mom, writer, and healthcare educator with a passion to create positive change. Born in Canada to Greek parents, she says that on frequent visits to Greece, "Mother Earth was forever imprinted in my cells, giving me a deep connection to nature." Her decision to have children and attempts to conceive first led her to explore a healthy lifestyle, and she quickly educated herself on all aspects of natural healthcare. She is a member of the Holistic Moms Network and Waldorf Education parents' groups. Maria believes in the power of moms supporting each other, and encourages mothers to trust their own intuition in caring for their children. She envisions a future where families are empowered and confident in following their inner wisdom, to raise their children in a conscious world.

Maria's website is www.lovecenteredparenting.com, where she blogs regularly about family life, and shares information about green products, links to useful articles, and weekly tips and meditations. For the past six years she has presented workshops to the community on topics including GMOs in our food, the commercialization of childhood, therapeutic essential oils, and tips for dealing with common health issues. During her outreach, she has been invited to share about her events by NPR News and other forms of media. Maria participated in a workshop with Dr. Michael Gaeta on vaccine awareness, has assisted in healing workshops, and has written for Wise Mom magazine. She lives on Long Island, where she practices independently as a paralegal. She loves to share all that she has gathered on her parenting journey, and finds her greatest fulfillment in simple moments spent with her family, especially in nature. She can be reached at lovecenteredparenting@gmail.com.